THE STATE OF THE EARTH ATLAS

THE STATE OF THE EARTH ATLAS
Edited by Joni Seager

A Pluto Project

A Touchstone Book
Published by Simon & Schuster Inc.
New York   London   Toronto   Sydney   Tokyo   Singapore

TOUCHSTONE/SIMON AND SCHUSTER
Simon & Schuster Building
Rockefeller Center
1230 Avenue of the Americas
New York, New York 10020

Text copyright © 1990 by Joni Seager
Maps and graphics © 1990 by Swanston Publishing Ltd., Derby

Simultaneously published in Great Britain
by Unwin Hyman Limited,
15–17 Broadwick Street, London W1V 1FP

Edited and coordinated by Anne Benewick

Design by Grundy & Northedge, London
Artwork by James Mills-Hicks, Andrea Fairbrass, Jacqueline Land
and Jeanne Radford for Swanston Graphics Ltd., Derby

Printed and bound in Hong Kong
by Mandarin Offset International (HK) Ltd.

This book is printed on paper made from pulp from Finland and
Sweden. It comes from managed forest, where the rate of replanting
means that timber stocks are rising.

10   9   8   7   6   5   4   3   2   1
10   9   8   7   6   5   4   3   2   1   Pbk.

Library of Congress Cataloging in Publication Data

The state of the earth atlas.

    "Simultaneously published in Great Britain by Unwin Hyman Limited"—
    Verso t.p.
    "A Pluto Project."
    Includes bibliographical references and index.
    Contents: Habitat earth—Food and water—Shelter—Energy—Industry—
    Defence—Consuming tastes—Green politics.
    1. Man—Influence on nature—Maps.   2. Natural resources—Maps.
    I. Seager, Joni.

G1046.G3S4   1990   333.7'0223   90-675120

ISBN 0-671-70523-7

ISBN 0-671-70524-5 (A Touchstone Book: pbk.)

CONTENTS

INTRODUCTION   11

1 A GLOBAL GREENHOUSE   16

HABITAT EARTH

2 A POPULAR PLANET   18
3 A SHRINKING WORLD   20
4 CUTTING OUR ROOTS   22
5 RAINFOREST   24

FOOD AND WATER

6   DRINKING WATER   26
7   HUNGER AND PLENTY   28
8   LIVING OFF THE LAND   30
9   THE CHEMICAL FIX   32
10 SHRINKING GENES   34
11 LOSING GROUND   36
12 FISHING FOR FOOD   38

SHELTER

13 CITY SPRAWL   40
14 COASTAL CRISIS   42
15 WASTE   44
16 SEWAGE   46
17 AIR QUALITY   48

ENERGY

18 ENERGY BUDGETS   50
19 THE NUCLEAR FAMILY   52
20 HYDRO POWER   54
21 FIREWOOD   56
22 OIL POLLUTION   58
23 FOSSIL FUEL POLLUTION   60
24 ACID RAIN   62

INDUSTRY

25 INDUSTRIAL WASTE   64
26 DEADLY INDUSTRY   66
27 TOXIC TRADE   68
28 HOLES IN THE SKY   70

DEFENCE

29 WAR-WASTED LANDS   72
30 NUCLEAR BLIGHT   74

CONSUMING TASTES

31 AUTO CULTURE   76
32 TOURIST TRAPS   78
33 THE WILD TRADE   80
34 HUNTING   82
35 THE TIMBER TRADE   84
36 PAYING THE PRICE   86

GREEN POLITICS

37 A CLASH OF INTERESTS   88
INTERNATIONAL TABLE   90

COMMENTARY   99

INDEX   125

EDITOR

JONI SEAGER is a Canadian geographer, currently living in the United States. She is a lecturer at the Massachusetts Institute of Technology and a member of the New Words feminist book collective. She is the co-author of *Women in the World: An International Atlas* and author of *Earth Follies: Making Feminist Sense of the Global Environment* (forthcoming).

CONTRIBUTORS

MARINA ALBERTI works on issues of hazardous waste management and environmental policy. She is a member of the Cooperativa Ecologia in Milan, where she participates actively in the environmental movement.

SIMON ALBRECHT is currently running the Data Support for Education service for the Nature Conservancy Council, Great Britain. He organised a seminar on Teaching Conservation in 1986 and has written two educational resource packs, *Pollution Facts* and *Conservation Facts* (1989).

MIKE BIRKIN has a long involvement with Friends of the Earth, UK and is currently their Regional Development Officer in London. Formerly an environmental consultant, he is co-author of *C is for Chemicals: Chemical Hazards and How to Avoid Them* (1989).

ANDY CRUMP has worked in various parts of the world as an ecologist, biological pest control specialist and writer on all aspects of environment and development. Formerly with the Panos Institute in London, he is currently a freelance writer/researcher in West Germany.

LESLEY DOWNING is a specialist in rural development who has worked in Kenya and the Philippines for seven years, administering community-based development programmes and including projects on small-scale rural water supply.

THOMAS E. DOWNING is a geographer who has conducted research on environmental issues, natural hazards, drought, famine and food policy in Africa, the USA and Mexico. He has spent four years in Kenya formulating district environmental policies.

NIGEL DUDLEY is an ecologist, specializing in pollution issues and the impact of Western institutions on the environment of the South. He works particularly with Earth Resources Research in London and the Soil Association in Bristol.

DOMINIC GOLDING is a Senior Research Associate at the Center for Technology, Environment and Development (CENTED), Clark University, Massachusetts. He is a geographer with research interests in the social aspects of risk assessment and hazard management.

LISA GREBER is a physicist and an activist who has worked on solar cell materials and citizens' control of nuclear power. She is currently acting director of Science for the People in Cambridge, Massachusetts.

CLAIRE HOLMAN is an independent environmental researcher working mainly on air pollution issues. She has worked as Information Officer for Friends of the Earth, UK and is currently adviser to both Friends of the Earth, UK and the Worldwide Fund for Nature, UK.

CONSTANCE E. HUNT is a biologist working for the US Army Corps of Engineers. She was previously a Research Associate at the National Wildlife Federation (US) and is the author of *Down by the River* (1988).

CHRISTINE LANCASTER is currently working as an Education Campaigner for the Parents Against Tobacco campaign (UK). Previously, she was a Research Associate on the Friends of the Earth Tropical Rain Forest Campaign.

JEAN MACRAE is an independent researcher in Boston, Massachusetts with an interest in public health. She is a founding member of the New Words Feminist Bookstore Collective.

JAN MCHARRY is currently Information Officer for Friends of the Earth, UK. Trained as an environmental resource planner, she has had a long involvement with grassroots environmental groups in the UK working on a range of environmental issues.

MICHAEL RENNER is a Senior Researcher at the Worldwatch Institute in Washington DC. He is working on environmental security issues.

MICHAEL SHANABROOK is a research assistant at the Congressional Budget Office in Washington DC. His research interests include the impact of global warming and international environmental treaty negotiations.

DAN SMITH is Associate Director of the Transnational Institute, Amsterdam and the author of several books on armament and disarmament. He is co-author with Michael Kidron of another Pluto Project, *The War Atlas* (1983), to appear in a second edition in 1991 as *The New Atlas of War and Peace*.

MICHAEL STEINITZ has taught urban and cultural geography and researched topics relating to past human environmental interactions. He is presently working in Massachusetts for the protection of historic built environments and sites.

ACKNOWLEDGEMENTS

For their assistance in providing information for individual maps, we would like to thank the following:

Hayward R. Alker, Jr., Massachusetts Institute of Technology, Cambridge, Mass.; Carl Bartone, World Bank, Washington DC; Margaret Bluman, London; Steven Broad, World Conservation Monitoring Centre, Cambridge, UK; Marva Coates, Food and Agriculture Organization, Washington DC; Peter Cebon, Massachusetts Institute of Technology, Cambridge, Mass.; Mark Davis, London; Stephen Davis, World Conservation Monitoring Centre, Surrey, UK; Cynthia Enloe, Clark University, Worcester, Mass.; Environmental Project on Central America (EPOCA); Joe Farman, British Antarctic Survey, Cambridge, UK; Paula Ferguson, Massachusetts Institute of Technology, Cambridge, Mass.; Hilary French, Worldwatch Institute, Washington DC; John Gille, National Center for Atmospheric Research, Colorado; Rupert Hastings, Royal Botanic Gardens, Surrey, UK; Norbert Henninger, World Resources Institute, Washington DC; Richard Hosier, University of Pennsylvania; Carol Inskipp, Worldwide Fund for Nature, Surrey, UK; Jodi Jacobson, Worldwatch Institute, Washington DC; Judy Johnson, Environmental Protection Agency, Washington DC; Peter Kearns, Department of the Environment, UK; Victoria Lane, Somerville, Mass.; Nick Lenssen, Worldwatch Institute, Washington DC; Christine Leon, World Conservation Monitoring Centre, Surrey, UK; Robert Mason, Temple University, Philadelphia; Alison McCusker, International Board for Plant Genetic Resources, Rome; Christine McGowan, Advisory Committee on Genetic Manipulation, UK; Arthur McKenzie, Tanker Advisory Center, New York City; Maldives Services Ltd, London; Norman Myers; Nature Conservancy Council, Data Support for Education Service, Peterborough, UK; Sam Ozolins, World Health Organization, Geneva; Steve Parcels, Natural Resources Defense Council, New York City; Bonnie Ram, Washington DC; Scott Saleska, Institute for Energy and Environmental Research, Takoma Park, Maryland; Cindy Pollock Shea, Worldwatch Institute, Washington DC; Seth Shulman, Science for the People, Cambridge, Mass.; Teresa Squires, American Cancer Society; Koy Thompson, Friends of the Earth, UK; World Action on Recycling Materials for Energy from Rubbish (WARMER), Tunbridge Wells, UK; Worldwide Fund for Nature, Data Support for Education Service, Surrey, UK; Worldwide Fund for Nature International, Switzerland.

INTRODUCTION

Concern is the catalyst that shapes this atlas. We share with many the belief that habitat earth, in the late 20th century, is in growing trouble. This is not really news; as the media, advertisers and even industry take up the 'green' cause, this unsettling assessment can scarcely have escaped the attention of many.

And yet much information about environmental matters remains confined to the privileged domain of specialists. Our purpose in undertaking this atlas is to translate specialist information into a form that can be more widely appreciated. As environmental consciousness grows to a popular groundswell, we need to be able to make sense of the mass of facts bombarding us from our newspapers and television screens. The need for a coherent overview of the state of the earth has never been greater, particularly so for information presented in an accessible and engaging manner.

In this atlas, we use the fact of environmental crisis not as an endpoint, but as the place from which to begin further enquiry. Not all parts of the global environment and not all places in the world are in the same state of distress. We ask where threats exist to a greater or lesser degree, and why they are so distributed. Most of the deterioration in our environment is the direct or indirect consequence of particular human arrangements of economic and political power, superimposed on vulnerable ecological systems. Not all economies nor all cultures, however, impose the same burdens on the environmental equilibrium. This atlas seeks to identify where such threats originate and why, indeed, they do so.

We encompass the state of the earth as broadly as possible. Thus, we offer information on issues that may already be familiar to many, such as ozone depletion, tropical rainforest destruction, and the plague of oil spills. But we also extend our reach to include topics that have received less popular attention, such as tourism, car culture, wetlands loss, and the international trade in tropical timber and in wildlife.

A primary truth of environmentalism is that everything is connected. The web of life is seamless, and the consequences of disruption to one part of the ecosystem ripple throughout the whole: soil erosion in the Himalayas contributes to massive flooding in Bangladesh, the deforestation of the Amazon may alter the atmospheric balance over the whole globe, and chemicals and gases produced in the richer industrial countries are destroying the ozone layer that protects everyone, rich and poor alike.

This interconnectedness makes it an excercise of frustration to arrange environmental topics in a clearly demarcated, apparently logical sequence. It should be understood that both sections and subject sequence in this atlas are largely artificial. The topics we have chosen are essentially part of a synergistic whole, wherein as much information can be gleaned from drawing comparisons and contrasts between maps as from studying them individually. The use of maps does, at least, facilitate such cross-referencing; continuities and contrasts become visible patterns on the page; threads of similarity and difference weave their way through the book.

It is a startling fact, which this atlas makes clear, that much environmental degradation transcends traditional economic and political boundaries. Environmental problems are much the same in centrally-controlled Communist states and 'free market' capitalist ones, in people's republics and diehard monarchies. The residents of Beijing and Paris suffer much the same levels of sulphur dioxide poisoning in the air they breathe; the impact of soil erosion is much the same whether in Jamaica or the USA; per head of population, Saudi Arabia, the UK and the USSR emit similar levels of carbon dioxide into the world's atmosphere; both the Aral Sea and the North Sea are dying because of the misplaced priorities of governments and industries, East and West.

When trying to make sense of environmental issues, the conventional way of conceptualizing world divisions by political boundaries seems inadequate. Dividing the world into communist and capitalist states, or free market and state-controlled economies, is of limited value in explaining the environmental state of the earth. More useful connections can be made between those countries that are fossil-fuel dependent and those that are hydro-dependent; or between those with and without tropical rainforest; or between those that produce CFCs and those that do not. By creating new links and categories of explanation in this atlas, we enable alliances to be reconceptualized: the USA and USSR have more in common than not, and the biggest blocs of environmental alliance are among rich and industrial nations and among poor and non-industrial ones.

New alliances based on environmental affinities and commonalities are already forming and will shape environmental politics into the next century. In 1989, the Maldives government hosted the first 'Small States Conference on Sea Level Rise', bringing together oceanic states that will be the first affected by global warming; in the late 1980s, a number of caucuses of poorer countries, including meetings of the Non-Aligned States, the Economic Community of West African States, and the Organization of African Unity, passed resolutions calling on industrialized countries to halt toxic waste dumping; and the '30 percent Club' has brought together those countries of Western Europe committed to cooperate in reducing sulphur dioxide emissions, the major cause of acid rain.

Certainly the weight of evidence underscores the responsibility of rich states for many of the global environmental problems we now face: the loss of animal, bird and plant species, fossil fuel pollution, the production and use of ozone-depleting chemicals, the ocean pollution that comes with oil dependency, the sulphur dioxide emissions that destroy forests and lakes, the stripping of tropical forests for timber and cattle-ranch farming - to name but a few. The catalogue of problems caused by the voracious resource appetites of the rich is almost overwhelming and the by-products are fouling our environment. The rich industrial world is stripping the earth of resources and in the course of so doing is generating enormous quantities of effluent and pollution that burden global ecosystems.

Rich countries continue to enhance their wealth by expanding their resource reach beyond their own borders while frequently exporting their problems. Having stripped their own forests, they are turning to timber-plundering in former colonies; choking on a glut of municipal, household and industrial garbage, they seek to ship away their waste to small Pacific islands or debt-strapped countries in Africa. But this is a small planet: there are limited resource frontiers to exploit - and there is no 'away'. There is no safe place to store carcinogenic chemicals, nuclear waste or the toxic by-products of industry. There is no safe way of dispersing CFCs or many of the other harmful gases being vented into the atmosphere. There are limits to global tolerance.

The global scale of this atlas makes powerful generalizations about the responsibilities of the rich world. It is less able to expose the local examples of environmental degradation that are all around us. Yet the destruction of wildlife habitat, the pollution of waterways and fuelwood scarcity – to name but a few issues – are often at their most serious at a regional or site-specific level.

On this smaller scale, it is important to recognize that the role of individuals in influencing environmental fates is mediated by, among other factors, gender, class, ethnicity and religion. Men and women, for example, have different relationships to the large institutions – governments, militaries, industrial corporations – that hold the balance of power on environmental issues. Similarly, the implications and experience of environmental decay are often different for men and women, rich and poor, elites and disenfranchized. Within a country, region or city, environmental degradation will be experienced differently, and more direly, by poor people living in slums with limited access to safe water, food and health care, than wealthier people insulated from environmental problems by their privilege.

The maps in this atlas inevitably focus on the physical form of environmental problems. With this in mind, in the Commentary to the maps (see page 99ff) we have tried wherever possible to discuss social, political and gender issues.

There are important environmental issues that, for one reason or another, do not appear in this atlas. Mining, perhaps because it includes a wide range of activities, defied our concept of global mapping even though it is a universally destructive enterprise, causing land degradation, pollution from tailings, chemical leaching, deforestation and landscape scarring. Although car culture and its concomitant air pollution are both included, the increasing density of road networks is omitted, for lack of appropriate global statistics. For similar reasons we do not map the spread of industrialization, the displacement of subsistence agriculture by cash cropping and luxury foods, the increasing numbers of environmental refugees, or grassroots mobilization to confront environmental problems.

Global information-gathering technology is proliferating. At the same time, access to and control of information is becoming more privatized. Full disclosure of environmental problems does not necessarily serve the purposes of the industries and governments that gather most environmental data. Without the untiring work of independent environmental groups such as the World Resources Institute, Greenpeace, Friends of the Earth and other international, national and community-based groups, we would know even less than we do about the state of the earth. We would like to think that this atlas will support and contribute to their efforts. An informed citizenry is the world's best hope.

The creation of this atlas drew on the goodwill and good sense of many dozens of individuals. I extend elsewhere our collective thanks to those who provided assistance with particular maps. I wish to single out for appreciation here a few brave souls who gave encouragement, criticism and invaluable support through every stage of this project. My greatest debt is to Anne Benewick, whose keen eye and wit shaped this project from its very beginning, and who shepherded it through all the editorial and production stages from mere doodles on paper to finished artwork and text. David Pratt made a valuable contribution in the formative stages of the project and Grundy & Northedge added their fine and distinctive design style. Swanston Graphics proved stellar, true to form, and an editor could not ask for a more competent and pleasant production and support team. Two project advisers, John Baines in the UK and Jeanne Kasperson of the Center for Technology, Environment & Development at Clark University, assisted in the early conceptualization of the project and, in particular, helped to assemble our research team.

Cynthia Enloe's unwavering support sustained me throughout the year-and-a-half that this atlas took over my life, and I have drawn heavily on her analytical acuity to steer a course through the intellectual maze of trying to make sense of the state of the earth. My colleagues in the New Words collective – Gilda Bruckman, Mary Lowry, Doris Reisig, Kate Rushin and Laura Zimmerman – tolerated my more-than-usual eccentricities and accommodated my absences with good humour.

The compilation of the research for this atlas was a collaborative effort in which I was aided by an able team of contributors who each provided not only specialist knowledge and timely insight, but a sense of camaraderie and shared purpose. The strength of this atlas rests on the firm research foundation which they built, map by map. For any errors that slipped into the presentation of their research, or for the liberties that I may have taken in its interpretation, I take sole responsibility.

Joni Seager
Somerville, Massachusetts
April 1990

Copyright © Swanston Publishing Limited

GREENLAND
(Den)

GREAT
BRITAIN
● Glasgow

● Liverpool

London ●

CANADA

NORWAY   SWEDEN

DENMARK Hamburg

Amsterdam/   BEL'N
Rotterdam   W.GER

FRANCE

Venice

PORTUGAL   SPAIN

San Francisco

UNITED STATES
OF AMERICA

Boston

New York

Los Angeles/
San Diego

New Orleans

BERMUDA

ATLANTIC
OCEAN

MOROCCO   TUNISIA

Miami

BAHAMAS

WESTERN SAHARA

ALGERIA   LIB

MEXICO

Veracruz

CUBA

BELIZE
HONDURAS

HAITI
DOMINICAN
REPUBLIC

JAMAICA   PUERTO RICO
(US)

ST.KITTS-
NEVIS

ST.VINCENT

ANTIGUA
GUADELOUPE (Fr)

MARTINIQUE (Fr)

BARBADOS

TRINIDAD &
TOBAGO

MAURITANIA   MALI   NIGER

Banjul/
Dakar

CAPE VERDE

GAMBIA   SENEGAL

GUINEA-BISSAU

SIERRA-LEONE   GUINEA
Freetown   IVORY
          LIBERIA COAST

Abidjan

GUATEMALA
EL SALVADOR

NICARAGUA

COSTA RICA

PANAMA

Caracas

VENEZUELA

SURINAME

GUYANA

FRENCH GUIANA (Fr)

Georgetown

BURKINA

GHANA
TOGO
BENIN

NIGERIA

Lagos

CAMEROON

EQUATORIAL GUINEA

SAO TOME & PRINCIPE

GABON   CONGO

COLOMBIA

ECUADOR

PERU

BRAZIL

ATLANTIC
OCEAN

PACIFIC
OCEAN

BOLIVIA

PARAGUAY

Rio de Janeiro

Walvis Bay

NAM

CHILE

URUGUAY

Buenos Aires

ARGENTINA   Montevideo

FALKLAND ISLANDS (Br)

A GLOBAL GREENHOUSE

AREAS VULNERABLE TO A RISE IN
SEA LEVEL AS A RESULT OF GLOBAL
WARMING

◉ coastal areas and
major cities

CLOSE-UPS
Bangladesh

☐ areas vulnerable to a rise
of 50 cms

■ areas vulnerable to a rise
of 1 metre

Great Britain

☐ areas vulnerable to a rise
of 1 metre

SMALL ISLANDS

● participants in Small States
Conference on Sea Level
Rise, Maldives *1989*

For carbon dioxide emissions see Map 23;
for other greenhouse gases see Map 17.

nitrous
oxides
6

other
12

CFCs
14

carbon dioxide
50

%

methane
18

Proportion of global warming attributed to individual gases mid-1980s

GREENHOUSE GASES

16

Data compiled by Nigel Dudley   Main sources: National Center for Atmospheric Research/National Science Foundation; World Resources Institute (1988); Hansen (1988).

Present evidence of global warming is controversial, but the implications could be so severe that the threat must be taken seriously.

UNION OF SOVIET SOCIALIST REPUBLICS

Odessa
Rostov
Astrakhan
MONGOLIA
BANGLADESH
Dalian
N KOREA
S KOREA
JAPAN
TURKEY
CYPRUS
LEBANON
ISRAEL
SYRIA
IRAQ
IRAN
AFGHANISTAN
JOR
Al Kuwyt
Abadan
PAKISTAN
Dhaka
PACIFIC OCEAN
BAHRAIN
QATAR
U.A.E
Ahmadabad
Karachi
GYPT
SAUDI ARABIA
OMAN
TAIWAN
Hong Kong
N
YEMEN
S YEMEN
DJIBOUTI
Rangoon
MYANMAR
THAILAND
UDAN
ETHIOPIA
Madras
Bangkok
CAM
VIETNAM
PHILIPPINES
ANDAMAN ISLANDS
Ho Chi Minh
SOMALIA
SRI LANKA
Male
MALDIVES
KENYA
UGANDA
Mugdisho
INDIAN OCEAN
BRUNEI
MALAYSIA
Singapore
INDONESIA
PAPUA NEW GUINEA
TANZANIA
Dar-es-Salaam
SEYCHELLES
Singapore
COMOROS
KIRIBATI
SOLOMON ISLANDS
TUVALU
WESTERN SAMOA
VANUATU
FIJI
TONGA

MALAWI
MADAGASCAR
Beira
MAURITIUS
MBABWE
MOZAMBIQUE
Maputo

AUSTRALIA
Sydney

NEW ZEALAND

COMPUTER SIMULATION OF THE EFFECT OF A FURTHER DOUBLING OF CARBON DIOXIDE IN THE ATMOSPHERE

areas that would be wetter than now

areas that would be drier than now

WORLD SCENARIO

POPULATIONS 1985

ANNUAL RATE OF
POPULATION CHANGE *1980-85*

- 3% increase
- 2%
- 1%
- decline

A POPULAR PLANET

COUNTRIES' SHARES OF WORLD
POPULATION *1985* AND OF
PROJECTED WORLD POPULATION
2025
size of country equals
size of population

100 million

10 million

POPULATIONS 2025

PROJECTED ANNUAL RATE OF
POPULATION CHANGE *2020-25*

- 2% increase
- 1%
- decline

Data compiled by Michael Steinitz   Main sources: UN *World Population Prospects* (1988).

The average person in the 'developed' world consumes 10 times as much energy and one-and-a-half times as much food – and produces 16 times as much air pollution – as the average person in the 'developing' world. The deterioration of the global environment has less to do with population growth than with industrial economies and priorities.

NORWAY
SWEDEN
FINLAND

GREENLAND
(Den)

UNITED
KINGDOM

IRELAND
NETH
DENMARK

WEST
GERMANY

CANADA

UNITED
STATES
OF AMERICA

FRANCE
AUSTRIA

PORTUGAL
SPAIN
ITALY

TURKEY

BAHAMAS

CUBA

JAMAICA

PUERTO
RICO (US)

MEXICO

GAMBIA

BELIZE

GUATEMALA

GUINE

EL SALVADOR
HONDURAS

SIERRA-
LEONE

NICARAGUA

TRINIDAD &
TOBAGO

CAPE VERDE

COSTA RICA

PANAMA

NETHERLANDS
ANTILLES

GUYANA

FRENCH
GUIANA
(Fr)

COLOMBIA
VENEZUELA

SURINAME

A SHRINKING WORLD

NUMBER OF KNOWN MAMMAL
SPECIES PER COUNTRY
1985 or latest year available
Size of country equals number of
species

ECUADOR
BRAZIL

100 species

1 species

PROPORTION OF MAMMAL
SPECIES UNDER THREAT OF
EXTINCTION
mid-1980s

PARAGUAY

PERU
BOLIVIA

30%

20%

10%

5%

URUGUAY

ARGENTINA

Extremes: São Tome, Netherlands Antilles
0% – France 52%

CHILE

For trade in wildlife see Map 33; for
hunting see Map 34; for whales see Map 34

Data compiled by Andy Crump   Main sources: IUCN Monitoring Centre (1988); OECD (1989); World Resources Institute (1987, 1988)

By the close of this century, 100 animal species
a day may be facing extinction.

EMPTY NESTS

PROPORTION OF BIRD SPECIES
UNDER THREAT OF EXTINCTION
OECD countries
mid-1980s

- 30%
- 20%
- 10%

data not available/other

Extremes: Australia, Canada 3.3% –
Austria 60.2%

CANADA

USA

FINLAND

NORWAY

SWEDEN

IRELAND

UNITED
KINGDOM

DENMARK

N

BEL

LUX

WEST
GERMANY

FRANCE

SWITZ

AUSTRIA

PORTUGAL

SPAIN

ITALY

JAPAN

AUSTRALIA

NEW ZEALAND

GUINEA-BISSAU

WESTERN
SAHARA

MOROCCO

MAURITANIA

MALI

BURKINA

ALGERIA

TUNISIA

LIBYA

EGYPT

NIGER

IVORY
COAST

GHANA

TOGO

BENIN

NIGERIA

SUDAN

ETHIOPIA

DJIBOUTI

CAMEROON

CHAD

UGANDA

SOMALIA

GABON

EQUATORIAL
GUINEA

CAR

RWANDA

KENYA

SAO TOME & PRINCIPE

CONGO

ZAIRE

BURUNDI

TANZANIA

ZAMBIA

MALAWI

ANGOLA

ZIMBABWE

NAMIBIA

BOTSWANA

MOZAMBIQUE

SOUTH
AFRICA

SWAZI
LAND

LES

JAPAN

AUSTRALIA

NEW ZEALAND

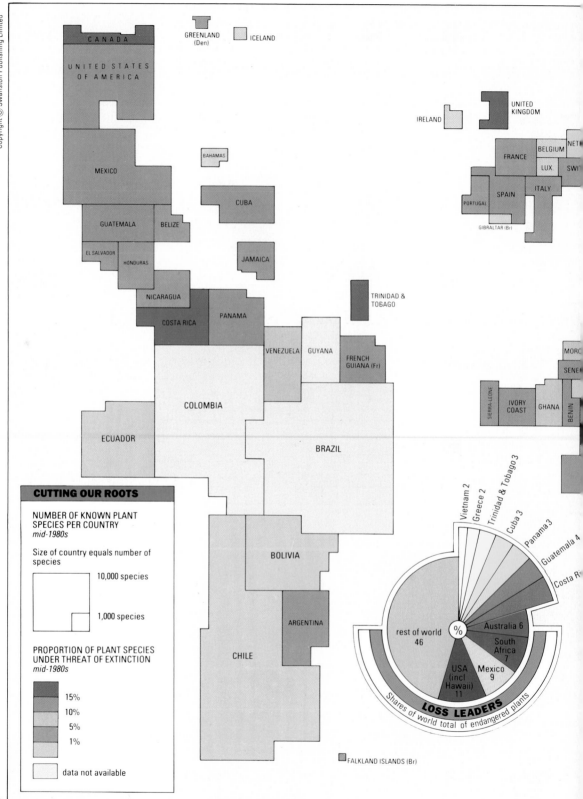

CANADA

UNITED STATES
OF AMERICA

GREENLAND
(Den)

ICELAND

MEXICO

BAHAMAS

CUBA

GUATEMALA

BELIZE

EL SALVADOR

HONDURAS

JAMAICA

NICARAGUA

COSTA RICA

PANAMA

VENEZUELA

GUYANA

FRENCH
GUIANA (Fr)

TRINIDAD &
TOBAGO

COLOMBIA

ECUADOR

BRAZIL

BOLIVIA

ARGENTINA

CHILE

IRELAND

UNITED
KINGDOM

NET

BELGIUM

FRANCE

LUX.

SWIT

PORTUGAL

SPAIN

ITALY

GIBRALTAR (Br)

MORO

SENE

SIERRA LEONE

IVORY
COAST

GHANA

BENIN

FALKLAND ISLANDS (Br)

CUTTING OUR ROOTS

NUMBER OF KNOWN PLANT
SPECIES PER COUNTRY
mid-1980s

Size of country equals number of
species

10,000 species

1,000 species

PROPORTION OF PLANT SPECIES
UNDER THREAT OF EXTINCTION
mid-1980s

15%

10%

5%

1%

data not available

LOSS LEADERS
Shares of world total of endangered plants

Vietnam 2
Greece 2
Trinidad & Tobago 3
Cuba 3
Panama 3
Guatemala 4
Costa Ri

rest of world
46

%

Australia 6

South
Africa
7

USA
(incl
Hawaii)
11

Mexico
9

Data compiled by Simon Albrecht   Main sources: Davis et al. (1979); World Resources Institute (1988).

Plants are the building blocks of all life on the planet.

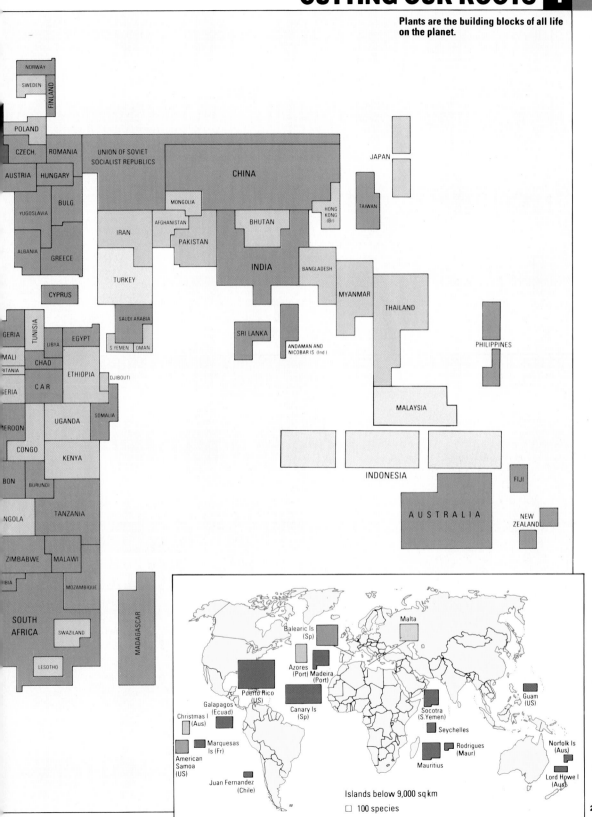

NORWAY

SWEDEN

FINLAND

POLAND

CZECH. | ROMANIA

AUSTRIA | HUNGARY

UNION OF SOVIET SOCIALIST REPUBLICS

CHINA

JAPAN

YUGOSLAVIA

BULG.

MONGOLIA

TAIWAN

ALBANIA | GREECE

IRAN

AFGHANISTAN

BHUTAN

HONG KONG (Br)

CYPRUS

TURKEY

PAKISTAN

INDIA

BANGLADESH

MYANMAR

THAILAND

SAUDI ARABIA

SRI LANKA

PHILIPPINES

GERIA | TUNISIA | EGYPT

LIBYA

S.YEMEN | OMAN

ANDAMAN AND NICOBAR IS (Ind.)

MALI

CHAD

RITANIA

ETHIOPIA

DJIBOUTI

GERIA | C A R

MALAYSIA

MEROON | UGANDA

SOMALIA

CONGO | KENYA

INDONESIA

FIJI

BON | BURUNDI

NGOLA | TANZANIA

AUSTRALIA

NEW ZEALAND

ZIMBABWE | MALAWI

IBIA | MOZAMBIQUE

SOUTH AFRICA | SWAZILAND

MADAGASCAR

LESOTHO

Balearic Is (Sp)

Malta

Azores (Port) | Madeira (Port)

Puerto Rico (US)

Guam (US)

Galapagos (Ecuad)

Canary Is (Sp)

Socotra (S.Yemen)

Christmas I (Aus)

Seychelles

Marquesas Is (Fr)

Rodrigues (Maur)

Norfolk Is (Aus)

American Samoa (US)

Mauritius

Lord Howe I (Aus)

Juan Fernandez (Chile)

Islands below 9,000 sq km

☐ 100 species

GREENLAND (Den)

ICELAND

CANADA

NORWAY

DENMARK

IRELAND UNITED NETH
KINGDOM

W GER
E GERP

FRANCE

ITALY

UNITED STATES
OF AMERICA

ATLANTIC
OCEAN

PORTUGAL   SPAIN

GIBRALTAR (Br)   TUNISIA

MOROCCO

@BERMUDA

ALGERIA   LIB

PACIFIC
OCEAN

MEXICO

WESTERN SAHARA

42% **6%**

BAHAMAS

CUBA   DOMINICAN REPUBLIC
HAITI   PUERTO RICO (US)
BELIZE   JAMAICA

MAURITANIA

MALI   NIGER

CAPE VERDE

SENEGAL
GAMBIA
GUINEA-BISSAU

GUATEMALA   HONDURAS
EL SALVADOR

18% **5%**
CENTRAL AMERCIA

NICARAGUA

COSTA RICA

PANAMA

COLOMBIA

•BARBADOS

GUINEA
SIERRA LEONE   IVORY
COAST   GHANA

BURKINA   BENIN

10% **0%**

LIBERIA

TOGO   NIGERIA   CAMEROON

42% **0%**   C

83% **76%**

VENEZUELA

GUYANA
SURINAME
FRENCH GUIANA (Fr)

82% **80%**

EQUATORIAL GUINEA

33% **14%**

ECUADOR

GABON   CONGO

ZA

75% **56%**

43% **9%**

83% **79%**

76% **42%**

ANGC

BRAZIL

ATLANTIC
OCEAN

74% **64%**
PERU

NAMI

90% **76%**

66% **33%**
BOLIVIA

CHILE

PARAGUAY

Wildlife habitat loss bar chart

Country	%
Liberia	87
India	80
Ivory Coast	79
Philippines	79
Madagascar	75
Thailand	74
Myanmar	71
Cameroon	59
Zaire	55
Indonesia	49

Wildlife habitat loss in rainforest
countries where known
1986 percentages

HOMELESS

URUGUAY

ARGENTINA

RAINFOREST

country with some tropical
rainforest *late 1980s*

other countries

RAINFOREST REMAINING
Proportion of original rainforest
remaining

late 1980s   by 2010

over 75%

50-75%

25-50%

FALKLAND ISLANDS (Br)

1% to 25%

Data compiled by Friends of the Earth/Christine Lancaster   Main sources: Campbell & Hammond (1989); Myers & Houghton (1989).

A hundred acres of tropical forest are
destroyed every minute.

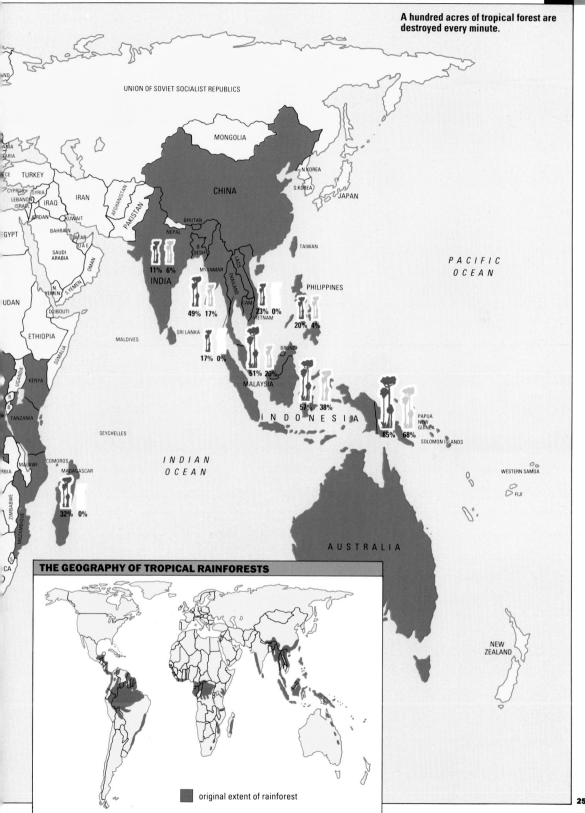

UNION OF SOVIET SOCIALIST REPUBLICS

MONGOLIA

CHINA

N.KOREA

S.KOREA

JAPAN

BHUTAN

NEPAL

B
DESH

MYANMAR

TAIWAN

*PACIFIC
OCEAN*

11% 6%

INDIA

49% 17%

THAILAND

LAOS

CAM

23% 0%
VIETNAM

PHILIPPINES

20% 4%

SRI LANKA

17% 0%

MALDIVES

BRUNEI

51% 20%

MALAYSIA

I N D O N E S I A

57% 38%

PAPUA
NEW
GUINEA

85% 68%

SOLOMON ISLANDS

SEYCHELLES

*INDIAN
OCEAN*

WESTERN SAMOA

FIJI

COMOROS

MADAGASCAR

32% 0%

AUSTRALIA

NEW
ZEALAND

TURKEY

CYPRUS

LEBANON
ISRAEL

SYRIA

IRAQ

IRAN

AFGHANISTAN

PAKISTAN

JORDAN

KUWAIT

BAHRAIN

EGYPT

QATAR

SAUDI
ARABIA

U.A.E

OMAN

N.
YEMEN

S.YEMEN

DJIBOUTI

UDAN

ETHIOPIA

SOMALIA

UGANDA

KENYA

TANZANIA

MALAWI

ZIMBABWE

MOZAMBIQUE

THE GEOGRAPHY OF TROPICAL RAINFORESTS

original extent of rainforest

GREENLAND
(Den)

ICELAND

NORWAY

SWEDEN

DENMARK

IRELAND UNITED
KINGDOM

NETH
BEL GER POL
W GER CZECH
FRANCE AUS
YUGOS

PORTUGAL SPAIN

ITALY

C A N A D A

TUNISIA

MOROCCO

ALGERIA LIBY

WESTERN SAHARA

UNITED STATES
OF AMERICA

BERMUDA

ATLANTIC
OCEAN

MAURITANIA MALI NIGER CHA

CAPE VERDE

SENEGAL
GAMBIA BURKINA
GUINEA-BISSAU NIGERIA
GUINEA
SIERRA LEONE IVORY GHANA BENIN
LIBERIA COAST
TOGO CAMEROON

MEXICO

BAHAMAS

CUBA HAITI DOMINICAN REPUBLIC
BELIZE PUERTO RICO (US)
HONDURAS JAMAICA
GUATEMALA GUADELOUPE (Fr)
EL SALVADOR DOMINICA
NICARAGUA MARTINIQUE (Fr)
BARBADOS
COSTA RICA TRINIDAD & TOBAGO
PANAMA

EQUATORIAL GUINEA
GABON
CONGO

VENEZUELA GUYANA
COLOMBIA SURINAME
FRENCH GUIANA (Fr)

ECUADOR

PERU

B R A Z I L

ATLANTIC
OCEAN

ANGO

BOLIVIA

PARAGUAY

NAMIBI

CHILE

URUGUAY

ARGENTINA

FALKLAND ISLANDS (Br)

DEMAND ON SUPPLY

How water is used
mid-1980s percentages

- agriculture
- industry
- domestic or public

	India	Mexico	Australia	USSR	Japan	USA	Canada	UK	W Germany	world average
	3	5	6	10	18	21	12	5		5
	4	7	16	17		49	70	79	22	22
	93	88	77	64	50	41	11	1	87	73

DRINKING WATER

PROPORTION OF POPULATION
WITH ACCESS TO SAFE DRINKING
WATER
mid-1980s percentages

- 25%
- 50%
- 75%
- data not available

CRISIS POINT

waterborne diseases
affecting more than 10% of
the population

Data compiled by Lesley Downing   Main sources: Goldsmith and Hildyard (1988); World Health Organization *Statistics Annual* (1986).

The availability of safe drinking water cannot be taken for granted, even in the 'developed' world.

UNION OF SOVIET SOCIALIST REPUBLICS

MONGOLIA

CHINA

TURKEY

CYPRUS
LEBANON
ISRAEL
SYRIA
JOR
IRAQ
IRAN
AFGHANISTAN
PAKISTAN
KUWAIT
BAHRAIN
QATAR
U.A.E.
EGYPT
SAUDI ARABIA
OMAN
N. YEMEN
S. YEMEN
DJIBOUTI

SUDAN
ETHIOPIA
SOMALIA
KENYA
TANZANIA
COMOROS
MALAWI
MADAGASCAR
ZIMBABWE
MOZAMBIQUE
SEYCHELLES
MALDIVES

N KOREA
S KOREA
JAPAN

TAIWAN

NEPAL
BHUTAN
INDIA
B
DESH
MYANMAR
LAOS
THAILAND
CAM
VIETNAM
SRI LANKA

PACIFIC
OCEAN

PHILIPPINES

BRUNEI
MALAYSIA
INDONESIA
KIRIBATI
TUVALU

PAPUA
NEW
GUINEA

WESTERN SAMOA
FIJI

AUSTRALIA

NEW
ZEALAND

PROPORTION OF POPULATION DRINKING REPROCESSED WASTE WATER

OECD countries
1987 percentages

- 90%
- 70%
- 50%

data not available/ other

DRINKING WASTE WATER

CANADA

U S A

IRELAND
UNITED KINGDOM
DENMARK
NORWAY
SWEDEN
FINLAND
N
BEL
LUX
WEST
GERMANY
FRANCE
SWITZ
AUSTRIA
PORTUGAL
SPAIN
ITALY

JAPAN

AUSTRALIA

AUSTRALIA

NEW ZEALAND

GREENLAND
(Den)

ICELAND

NORWAY

SWEDEN

DENMARK

UNITED
KINGDOM

IRELAND

NETH
BEL
L GER
W GER

E
GER

POL

CZECH
AUS
YUGOS

FRANCE

SWITZ

ITALY

C A N A D A

UNITED STATES
OF AMERICA

BERMUDA

ATLANTIC
OCEAN

PORTUGAL

SPAIN

TUNISIA

MOROCCO

ALGERIA

LIBY

WESTERN SAHARA

MEXICO

BAHAMAS

CUBA

HAITI

DOMINICAN REPUBLIC
PUERTO RICO (US)

BELIZE

HONDURAS

JAMAICA

GUADELOUPE (Fr)

DOMINICA

MARTINIQUE (Fr)

BARBADOS

TRINIDAD & TOBAGO

GUATEMALA

NICARAGUA

CAPE VERDE

MAURITANIA

MALI

NIGER

CH

SENEGAL

GAMBIA

GUINEA-BISSAU

GUINEA

BURKINA

SIERRA LEONE

IVORY
COAST

GHANA

BENIN

NIGERIA

LIBERIA

TOGO

CAMEROON

COSTA RICA

EL SALVADOR

PANAMA

VENEZUELA

GUYANA

SURINAME

FRENCH GUIANA (Fr)

COLOMBIA

EQUATORIAL GUINEA

SAO TOME & PRINCIPE

GABON

CONGO

ECUADOR

PERU

B R A Z I L

ATLANTIC
OCEAN

ANGO

BOLIVIA

PARAGUAY

NAMIB

CHILE

PACIFIC
OCEAN

URUGUAY

ARGENTINA

FALKLAND ISLANDS (Br)

HUNGER AND PLENTY

DISRUPTION OF FOOD SUPPLIES
1985-87

severe drought

famine

famine, exacerbated
by war

food supplies disrupted by
war, often intentionally

Data compiled by Jeanne Kasperson and Joni Seager   Main sources: FAO *Production Statistics* (1987); Kates (1989).

The persistence of hunger in a world of plenty represents the failure of social and economic systems.

UNION OF SOVIET SOCIALIST REPUBLICS

MONGOLIA

CHINA

N KOREA

S KOREA

JAPAN

PACIFIC OCEAN

TURKEY

LEBANON
SYRIA
ISRAEL JOR
IRAQ

IRAN

AFGHANISTAN

KUWAIT
BAHRAIN
QATAR
U.A.E.
OMAN

PAKISTAN

NEPAL BHUTAN

INDIA

B DESH

MYANMAR

LAOS

TAIWAN

HONG KONG (Br)

EGYPT

SAUDI ARABIA

N S YEMEN
YEMEN

THAILAND

VIETNAM

PHILIPPINES

S U D A N

DJIBOUTI

SRI LANKA

CAMBODIA

ETHIOPIA

SOMALIA

MALDIVES

BRUNEI

UGANDA

KENYA

M A L A Y S I A

IRE

SINGAPORE

TANZANIA

SEYCHELLES

INDIAN OCEAN

I N D O N E S I A

PAPUA NEW GUINEA

COMOROS

MADAGASCAR

MBIA

MALAWI

ZIMBABWE

MOZAMBIQUE

UTH RICA

SWAZILAND

WESTERN SAMOA

FIJI

A U S T R A L I A

NEW ZEALAND

HUNGER AND PLENTY

FOOD AVAILABLE PER PERSON COMPARED WITH WORLD AVERAGE
mid-1980s percentages

above average

more than 20% above

10 to 20%

up to 10%

world average

below average

up to 10% below

10 to 20%

more than 20% below average

data not available

Copyright © Swanston Publishing Limited

GREENLAND
(Den)

ICELAND

CANADA

UNITED STATES
OF AMERICA

NORWAY
SWEDEN
DENMARK
IRELAND UNITED
KINGDOM
NETH
BEL
E.GER
POLA
W.GER CZECH
AUS HUN
FRANCE
YUGOSLA
ITAL
PORTUGAL SPAIN

MEXICO

BERMUDA

ATLANTIC
OCEAN

BAHAMAS

CUBA
HAITI
DOMINICAN REPUBLIC
PUERTO RICO (US)
BELIZE
GUATEMALA HONDURAS JAMAICA
EL SALVADOR
GUADELOUPE (Fr)
NICARAGUA
DOMINICA
MARTINIQUE (Fr)
BARBADOS
COSTA RICA
TRINIDAD & TOBAGO
PANAMA

VENEZUELA
GUYANA
SURINAME
COLOMBIA
FRENCH GUIANA (Fr)

ECUADOR

PERU

B R A Z I L

MOROCCO
TUNISIA

ALGERIA
LIBYA

WESTERN SAHARA

MAURITANIA
MALI
NIGER
CHA

CAPE VERDES
SENEGAL
GAMBIA
GUINEA-BISSAU
BURKINA
GUINEA
NIGERIA
SIERRA LEONE IVORY
COAST
BENIN
LIBERIA
GHANA
TOGO
CAMEROON
EQUATORIAL GUINEA
C A
SAO TOME & PRINCIPE
GABON
CONGO

ANGO

PACIFIC
OCEAN

BOLIVIA

PARAGUAY

NAMIBIA

CHILE

URUGUAY

ARGENTINA

FALKLAND ISLANDS (Br)

LIVING OFF THE LAND

NUMBER OF PEOPLE SUPPORTED
PER HECTARE OF CROPLAND
1987
1 hectare = 2.47 acres

	10
	8
	5
	2
	data not available

World average: 3.5 people per hectare.

For food supply see Map 7; for
soil loss see Map 11.

Data compiled by Michael Shanabrook   Main sources: FAO, *Production Statistics Yearbook* (1989); Gramfors (1989); Kurian (1984).

LIVING OFF THE LAND 8

Agricultural land per person is shrinking the world over, although pressure on the land is not evenly distributed.

UNION OF SOVIET SOCIALIST REPUBLICS

MONGOLIA

N KOREA
S KOREA

JAPAN

TURKEY

CYPRUS
LEBANON
ISRAEL
JOR
IRAQ
SYRIA

AFGHANISTAN

CHINA

PACIFIC
OCEAN

EGYPT

KUWAIT
BAHRAIN
QATAR
U.A.E
OMAN

IRAN

PAKISTAN

NEPAL
BHUTAN

INDIA

B
DESH

TAIWAN

SAUDI ARABIA

N
YEMEN
S.YEMEN

MYANMAR

LAOS

SUDAN

DJIBOUTI

ETHIOPIA

SOMALIA

MALDIVES

THAILAND

CAM
VIETNAM

PHILIPPINES

SRI LANKA

BRUNEI

MALAYSIA

SINGAPORE

UGANDA
KENYA

IRE

SEYCHELLES

INDONESIA

PAPUA
NEW
GUINEA

TANZANIA

COMOROS

INDIAN OCEAN

MALAWI

IBIA

ZIMBABWE

MADAGASCAR

WESTERN SAMOA

FIJI

MOZAMBIQUE

UTH
RICA

AUSTRALIA

A NARROW MARGIN
Suitability of the world's land for agriculture

suitable for agriculture
11

permafrost 6

too wet
10

too dry
28

%

soil too
shallow
22

chemical
problems
23

unsuitable for agriculture

NEW
ZEALAND

31

ICELAND

FINLAND

NORWAY
SWEDEN

DENMARK

USSR

IRELAND

UNITED
KINGDOM

EAST
GERMANY

POLAND

NETH.

WEST
GERMANY

CZECHOSLOVAKIA

BEL.
LUX.

FRANCE

AUSTRIA

HUNG.

SWITZ.

ROMANI

YUGOSLAVIA

ITALY

BULG

ALBANIA

PORTUGAL

GREECE

SPAIN

GIBRALTAR (Br)

C A N A D A

UNITED STATES
OF AMERICA

ATLANTIC
OCEAN

BERMUDA

MOROCCO

TUNISIA

ALGERIA

LIBY

MEXICO

BAHAMAS

WESTERN SAHARA

CUBA

HAITI

DOMINICAN REPUBLIC
PUERTO RICO (US)

BELIZE

JAMAICA

GUATEMALA

HONDURAS

GUADELOUPE (Fr)

DOMINICA

MARTINIQUE (Fr)

MAURITANIA

MALI

NIGER

EL SALVADOR

NICARAGUA

BARBADOS

CAPE VERDE

SENEGAL

BURKINA

CHA

TRINIDAD & TOBAGO

GAMBIA

COSTA RICA

PANAMA

VENEZUELA

GUYANA

GUINEA-BISSAU

GUINEA

NIGERIA

SURINAME

IVORY
COAST

GHANA

BENIN

COLOMBIA

FRENCH GUIANA (Fr)

SIERRA LEONE

LIBERIA

CA

ECUADOR

TOGO

CAMEROON

PACIFIC
OCEAN

EQUATORIAL GUINEA

SAO TOME & PRINCIPE

GABON

CONGO

PERU

B R A Z I L

ATLANTIC
OCEAN

ANGO

BOLIVIA

NAMIBIA

PARAGUAY

CHILE

URUGUAY

ARGENTINA

THE CHEMICAL FIX

USE OF ARTIFICIAL FERTILIZERS IN
AGRICULTURE
1987 kg per hectare of arable land
1 kg = 2.2 lbs

extreme dependence
above 150 kg per hectare

heavy users
75-150 kg per hectare

dependent
10-75 kg per hectare

low users
below 10 kg per hectare

data not available

USE OF PESTICIDES IN
AGRICULTURE *1987*

heavy users of pesticides

FALKLAND ISLANDS (Br)

16,000

15,000

6000

3600

Sri Lanka

El Salvador

Montevideo

Cairo

Cases of pesticide poisoning
annual average *mid-1980s*

POISONINGS

32

Data compiled by Joni Seager   Main sources: FAO *Fertilizer Yearbook* (1988); FAO *Production Yearbook* (1987); FAO *Trade Statistics* (1988).

The more agricultural chemicals are
used, the more they are needed.

UNION OF SOVIET SOCIALIST REPUBLICS

MONGOLIA

N KOREA

JAPAN

S.KOREA

TURKEY

CYPRUS
LEBANON
ISRAEL JOR
SYRIA
IRAQ
KUWAIT
BAHRAIN
QATAR
U.A.E
OMAN

EGYPT

SAUDI ARABIA

IRAN

AFGHANISTAN

PAKISTAN

C H I N A

TAIWAN

PACIFIC
OCEAN

NEPAL
BHUTAN
B
DESH
MYANMAR
LAOS
THAILAND
CAM
VIETNAM

HONG KONG (Br)

PHILIPPINES

I N D I A

N
YEMEN
S YEMEN
DJIBOUTI

SUDAN

ETHIOPIA

SOMALIA

UGANDA
KENYA

RE
B

TANZANIA

SRI LANKA

MALDIVES

INDIAN OCEAN

SEYCHELLES

BRUNEI

M A L A Y S I A

SINGAPORE

I N D O N E S I A

PAPUA
NEW
GUINEA

COMOROS

BIA
MALAWI
ZIMB

MADAGASCAR

MOZAMBIQUE

JTH
ICA

WESTERN SAMOA

AUSTRALIA

FIJI

PUSHERS

USSR

CANADA

19

USA

17   30

UNITED
KINGDOM

13   4   7

NETH
B
W.GER
FRANCE
S
ROMANIA

3   6   5   20   3

10

8

E.GER

ISRAEL

3

USSR

12

JAPAN

5

NEW
ZEALAND

major exporters of artificial
fertilizers

major exporters of
pesticides

Copyright © Swanston Publishing Limited

FACTORY-FRESH

Releases of genetically-engineered organisms 1986-89

USA	26
France	19
UK	15
Belgium	5

grapes
V. amurensis
V. aestivalis
V. berlandieri
V. lincecumii
V. riparia
V. rupestris

carrot
Daucus carota

maize
T. dactyloides

sunflower
H. annuus
H. petiolaris

potato
S. demissum
S. stoloniferum

sweet potato
I. trifida

maize
T. dactyloides

maize
T. dactyloides

wheat
Ae. ventricosa

oats
A. sterilis

oats
A. sterilis

oats
A. sterilis

sugar beet
B. maritima

wheat
Ae. ventric

oil palm
E. guineensis

oil palm
E. guineensis

tomato
L. esculentum cerasiforme
L. Cheesmanii
L. pimpinellifolium
L. hirsutum

tomato
L. esculentum cerasiforme
L. pimpinellifolium
L. chmieleswkii
L. hirsutum
L. peruvianum

cacao
theobroma C.

cassava
M. gluzovii

potato
S. acaule

potato
S. acaule

potato
S. acaule
S. spegazzinii
S. vernei

tomato
L. peruvianum

SHRINKING GENES

SOURCES OF WILD GENES FOR IMPROVEMENT AND PROTECTION OF WORLD FOOD SUPPLIES

source of genes for major crop

critical areas for collection

STAPLE SUPPLIES

WHERE THE WORLD'S MAJOR FOOD CROPS ARE GROWN
mid-1980s percentages

'developed' countries

'developing' countries

wheat   rice   maize   barley   oats

34

Data compiled by Simon Albrecht   Main sources: Prescott-Allen (1988); Myers (1984)

There is no such thing as self-sufficiency in genetic resources. The world's food supplies depend on cooperative protection of the global gene pool of wild plants.

GREENLAND
(Den)

ICELAND

C A N A D A

NORWAY

SWEDEN

DENMARK

IRELAND

UNITED
KINGDOM

NETH.
BEL.

E.
GER

PO

W GER

CZECH

AUS.

H

FRANCE

YUGOS

ITALY

PORTUGAL

SPAIN

UNITED STATES
OF AMERICA

MOROCCO

TUNISIA

ALGERIA

L I B Y

WESTERN SAHARA

BERMUDA

ATLANTIC
OCEAN

MEXICO

BAHAMAS

CUBA

MAURITANIA

M A L I

N I G E R

HAITI
JAMAICA

DOMINICAN REPUBLIC
PUERTO RICO (US)

CAPE VERDE

SENEGAL

BELIZE
HONDURAS

GUATEMALA
EL SALVADOR

NICARAGUA

GUADELOUPE (Fr)

DOMINICA

MARTINIQUE (Fr)

BARBADOS

TRINIDAD & TOBAGO

GAMBIA

GUINEA-BISSAU

GUINEA

BURKINA

CH

SIERRA LEONE

IVORY
COAST

GHANA

BENIN

NIGERIA

TOGO

COSTA RICA

PANAMA

VENEZUELA

GUYANA

SURINAME

FRENCH GUIANA (Fr)

LIBERIA

CAMEROON

COLOMBIA

EQUATORIAL GUINEA

SAO TOME & PRINCIPE

GABON

ECUADOR

CONGO

PERU

B R A Z I L

ATLANTIC
OCEAN

ANG

BOLIVIA

PARAGUAY

NAMIB

CHILE

URUGUAY

PACIFIC
OCEAN

ARGENTINA

FALKLAND ISLANDS (Br)

LOSING GROUND

AREAS AT RISK OF
DESERTIFICATION
late 1980s

existing desert

very high risk

high risk

moderate risk

other land

severe land erosion

Data compiled by Andy Crump   Main sources: UNEP *World Conservation Strategy* (1980); World Resources Institute (1988); Myers (1984).

By the year 2000 one-third of the world's
agricultural land will have turned to dust.

UNION OF SOVIET SOCIALIST REPUBLICS

MONGOLIA

CHINA

TURKEY

CYPRUS
LEBANON
ISRAEL JOR
IRAQ
SYRIA
IRAN
AFGHANISTAN

KUWAIT
PAKISTAN
NEPAL
BHUTAN

EGYPT
BAHRAIN
QATAR
U.A.E.
SAUDI ARABIA
OMAN
INDIA
B
DESH
MYANMAR
LAOS

N KOREA
S KOREA
JAPAN

TAIWAN

PACIFIC
OCEAN

SUDAN
N
YEMEN
S YEMEN
DJIBOUTI
THAILAND
CAM
VIETNAM

ETHIOPIA
SOMALIA
PHILIPPINES

UGANDA
KENYA
SRI LANKA
MALDIVES

BRUNEI
MALAYSIA
SINGAPORE

RE
B
SEYCHELLES
TANZANIA
COMOROS

INDONESIA

PAPUA
NEW
GUINEA

BIA
MALAWI
ZIMBABWE
MOZAMBIQUE
MADAGASCAR

WESTERN SAMOA
FIJI

JTH
ICA
S

AUSTRALIA

LAND SLIDE

Percentage of land affected by soil
erosion *late 1980s*

Nepal	95
Peru	95
Turkey	95
Lesotho	88
Madagascar	79
Ethiopia	53
India	27
Thailand	25
Jamaica	19
USA	19
USSR	10
China	6
Nigeria	1

NEW
ZEALAND

FISHING FOR FOOD

FISH SUPPLY AVAILABLE PER
PERSON PER YEAR
mid-1980s kgs.

- 25
- 15
- 10
- 5

data not available

● major importers of fish

● major exporters of fish

STATUS OF MAJOR FISHING
GROUNDS
mid-1980s

◀┼┼┼ already severely depleted

intensively exploited

severely polluted

For wetlands loss see Map 14.

salmon *pollack*

halibut

perch

cod

haddock

Atlantic herring

anchovy

pilchard

Atlantic herring

CANADA

UNITED STATES
OF AMERICA

PACIFIC
OCEAN

ATLANTIC
OCEAN

MEXICO
CUBA
BAHAMAS
DOMINICAN REPUBLIC
PUERTO RICO (US)
JAMAICA GUADELOUPE (Fr)
BELIZE
HONDURAS DOMINICA
GUATEMALA MARTINIQUE (Fr)
EL SALVADOR BARBADOS
NICARAGUA
COSTA RICA TRINIDAD & TOBAGO
PANAMA
VENEZUELA GUYANA
COLOMBIA SURINAME
FRENCH GUIANA (Fr)
ECUADOR
PERU BRAZIL
BOLIVIA
PARAGUAY
CHILE
URUGUAY
ARGENTINA
FALKLAND ISLANDS (Br)

BERMUDA

ICELAND
NORWAY
SWEDEN
FINL
IRELAND
UNITED
KINGDOM
NETH
BEL E GER POLAND
FRANCE W GER CZECH
SWITZ AUSTRIA HUNG
ITALY YUGOSLAVIA
PORTUGAL SPAIN AL
ROM
BL
GREECE
MOROCCO ALGERIA TUNISIA

MOROCCO
ALGERIA LI
WESTERN SAHARA
MAURITANIA MALI NIGER
CAPE VERDE SENEGAL
GAMBIA
GUINEA-BISSAU BURKINA
GUINEA NIGERIA
SIERRA LEONE IVORY BENIN
COAST GHANA CAMEROON
LIBERIA TOGO
EQUATORIAL GUINEA
SAO TOME & PRINCIPE GABON CONGO
ANGO
NAMI
SO

Data compiled by Andy Crump   Main sources: FAO *Fishery Statistics* (1986, 1987); Myers (1984).

Fisheries provide almost a quarter of the world's supply of animal protein, but face threats from many sources.

UNION OF SOVIET SOCIALIST REPUBLICS

MONGOLIA

TURKEY
CYPRUS
SYRIA
LEBANON
ISRAEL
IRAN
IRAQ
KUWAIT
BAHRAIN
QATAR
U.A.E.
OMAN
SAUDI ARABIA
YEMEN
S YEMEN
JORDAN
GYPT
DJIBOUTI
ETHIOPIA
SOMALIA
UGANDA
KENYA
TANZANIA
COMOROS
MALAWI
ZIMBABWE
MOZAMBIQUE
MADAGASCAR

AFGHANISTAN
PAKISTAN
CHINA
NEPAL
BHUTAN
B'DESH
INDIA
MYANMAR
LAOS
THAILAND
CAM
VIETNAM
SRI LANKA
MALDIVES
SEYCHELLES

N KOREA
S KOREA
JAPAN
pollack

HONG KONG (Br)
TAIWAN

PHILIPPINES

BRUNEI
MALAYSIA
SINGAPORE
INDONESIA
PAPUA NEW GUINEA
SOLOMON ISLANDS

mackerel

PACIFIC OCEAN

INDIAN OCEAN

WESTERN SAMOA
FIJI

AUSTRALIA

TRAWLING TROUBLE

ICELAND
NORWAY
DENMARK
CANADA
USA
BERMUDA
PANAMA
LIBERIA
PERU
CHILE

E GER
SPAIN
POLAND
UNION OF SOVIET SOCIALIST REPUBLICS
CHINA
INDIA
JAPAN
KOREA
TAIWAN
INDONESIA
NEW ZEALAND

ATLANTIC OCEAN
PACIFIC OCEAN
INDIAN OCEAN
ATLANTIC OCEAN

MAJOR THREATS TO THE WORLD'S FISHERIES

- major factory-fishing countries
- major driftnet fishing countries
- both
- major driftnet fishing grounds
- other driftnet fishing grounds

Data compiled by Michael Steinitz   Main sources: UN *Prospects of World Urbanization* (1988); *National Geographic* (1984).

By the year 2000, half the world's
population will live in cities.

UNION OF SOVIET SOCIALIST REPUBLICS

Kiev

MONGOLIA

CHINA

Zibo

Seoul

N KOREA

S KOREA

JAPAN

Ankara

TURKEY

CYPRUS

LEBANON

SYRIA

IRAQ

JOR

ISRAEL

Tehran

Pusan

AFGHANISTAN

Baghdad

KUWAIT

IRAN

Chengdu

PACIFIC
OCEAN

Lahore

Delhi

Taipei

TAIWAN

Karachi

PAKISTAN

NEPAL

BHUTAN

Dhaka

BAHRAIN

QATAR

U.A.E

OMAN

SAUDI ARABIA

Kanpur

Ahmadabad

INDIA

Poona

MYANMAR

LAOS

HONG KONG (Br)

EGYPT

S YEMEN

YEMEN

N

S

Bombay

Hyderabad

Rangoon

Manila

SUDAN

ETHIOPIA

SOMALIA

Bangalore

Madras

THAILAND

CAM

VIETNAM

Bangkok

PHILIPPINES

DJIBOUTI

UGANDA

KENYA

SRI LANKA

MALDIVES

Singapore

BRUNEI

RE

TANZANIA

SEYCHELLES

INDIAN   OCEAN

Medan

SINGAPORE

MALAYSIA

INDONESIA

PAPUA
NEW
GUINEA

COMOROS

BA

MALAWI

MADAGASCAR

ZIMBABWE

RANKINGS OF THE WORLD'S
MAJOR CITIES BY SIZE

in 1960

in 1980

by 2000
based on current
growth rates

Jakarta

WESTERN SAMOA

FIJI

PRESSURE POINTS

New York/
NE New Jersey

Rhine/Ruhr

2

5

7

10

27

29

London

10

Moscow

16

22

AUSTRALIA

9

9

18

1

2

6

Paris

7

13

25

33

15

7

3

1

3

Tokyo-
Yokohama

Seoul

Los Angeles/
Long Beach

20

19

12

Cairo

16

19

5

Bombay

14

8

4

Calcutta

4

6

8

Shanghai

15

3

1

Mexico City

17

4

2

São Paulo

16

11

9

Rio de Janeiro

8

6

11

Buenos Aires

NEW
ZEALAND

BIRDS AT RISK

NUMBER OF BIRD
SPECIES AT RISK FROM
MANGROVE
DESTRUCTION
late 1980s

Seychelles	Venezuela	USA (Florida)	Trinidad & Tobago	Malaysia	Puerto Rico
2	3	5	8	9	34

COASTAL CRISIS

DISTRIBUTION OF MAJOR
MANGROVE WETLANDS
mid-1980s sq kms

- 5000
- 1000
- 100

size of mangrove wetlands unknown

countries with other major wetlands

other countries

THREATS TO MANGROVE
WETLANDS

urban and agricultural encroachment

mining and logging

pollution, oil spills, waste dumping

57 West Germany
55 Netherlands
42 Malaysia
29 Brunei
22 Finland
12 USA
9 Sweden

Proportion of wetlands
destroyed since 1950
percentages

WETLANDS LOSS

42

Data compiled by Michael Steinitz   Main sources: Saenger (1983); AMBIO (1988).

The world's wetlands are being drained and paved over for development. More than half have already been destroyed.

UNION OF SOVIET SOCIALIST REPUBLICS

MONGOLIA

CHINA

N KOREA

S KOREA

JAPAN

PACIFIC OCEAN

TURKEY

CYPRUS
LEBANON
ISRAEL
JOR
IRAQ

SYRIA

IRAN

AFGHANISTAN

EGYPT

KUWAIT

QATAR
UAE

OMAN

PAKISTAN

NEPAL

BHUTAN

TAIWAN

SAUDI ARABIA

N
YEMEN

S YEMEN

DJIBOUTI

INDIA

BANGLA
DESH

MYANMAR

LAOS

THAILAND

CAM

VIETNAM

PHILIPPINES

SUDAN

ETHIOPIA

SOMALIA

MALDIVES

SRI LANKA

BRUNEI

MALAYSIA

UGANDA

KENYA

SEYCHELLES

INDIAN OCEAN

SINGAPORE

INDONESIA

PAPUA
NEW
GUINEA

TANZANIA

RE

THE GEOGRAPHY OF THE WETLANDS

MALAWI

BIA

ZIMBABWE

MOZAMBIQUE

UTH
RICA

WESTERN SAMOA

FIJI

AUSTRALIA

ATLANTIC
OCEAN

PACIFIC
OCEAN

PACIFIC
OCEAN

ATLANTIC
OCEAN

INDIAN
OCEAN

NEW
ZEALAND

PACIFIC
OCEAN

▓ extent of major wetlands

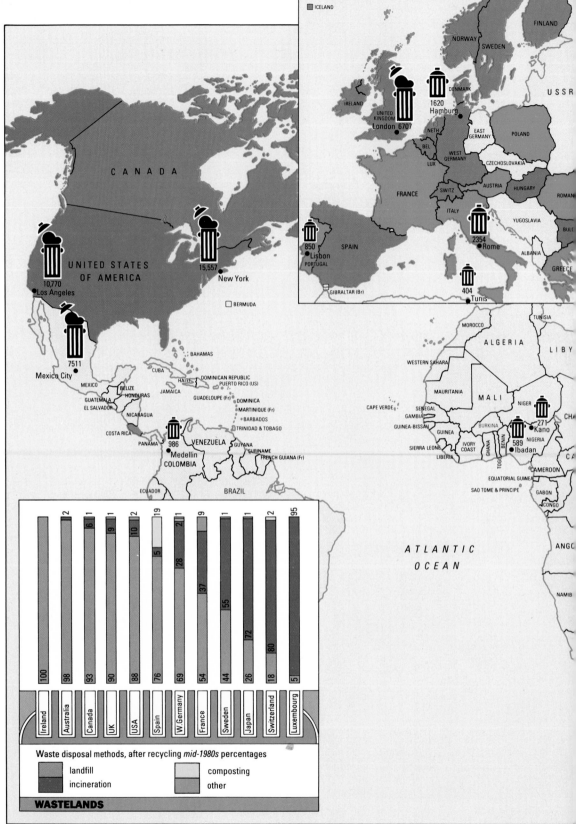

Copyright © Swanston Publishing Limited

□ ICELAND

1620
Hamburg

London 6707

850
Lisbon

2354
Rome

404
Tunis

CANADA

UNITED STATES
OF AMERICA

15,557
New York

10,770
Los Angeles

7511
Mexico City

□ BERMUDA

986
Medellin
COLOMBIA

271
Kano

589
Ibadan

ATLANTIC
OCEAN

Waste disposal methods, after recycling _mid-1980s_ percentages

Country	landfill	incineration	composting	other
Ireland	100			
Australia	98			2
Canada	93	6		1
UK	90	9		1
USA	88	10		2
Spain	76		5	19
W.Germany	69	28	2	1
France	54	37	9	
Sweden	44	55		1
Japan	26	72		1
Switzerland	18	80		2
Luxembourg	5			95

landfill

incineration

composting

other

WASTELANDS

44

Data compiled by Joni Seager   Main sources: Cointreau (1987); Levenson, US Congress Office of Technology Assessment; OECD _Environmental Data Compendium_ (1989).

The richer the country the more garbage it produces. But getting rid of it safely is a global problem.

Australia 1.1
France 1.5
UK 1.8
Canada 1.8
W. Germany 2.9
S. Korea 2.9
Japan 4.4

rest of world 64.6

%

USA 19.0

THROWAWAY SOCIETIES
Shares of total world waste mid-1980s

UNION OF SOVIET SOCIALIST REPUBLICS

TURKEY
CYPRUS
LEBANON
SYRIA
ISRAEL
JOR
IRAQ
IRAN
AFGHANISTAN
CHINA
N KOREA
Tokyo 9189
JAPAN
S.KOREA

PACIFIC
OCEAN

exandria
KUWAIT
BAHRAIN
QATAR
U.A.E.
EGYPT
1759
Amman
414
SAUDI ARABIA
OMAN

Lahore
2494
PAKISTAN
Karachi

NEPAL
BHUTAN
1020 Kanpur
INDIA
B
DESH
Calcutta
3088

MYANMAR
LAOS
THAILAND
CAM
VIETNAM

Hong
Kong
5586
TAIWAN

Manila 1134

PHILIPPINES

5646

SRI LANKA

MALDIVES

N
YEMEN
S YEMEN
DJIBOUTI

UDAN
ETHIOPIA
SOMALIA

UGANDA
KENYA

RE

TANZANIA

SEYCHELLES

COMOROS

RIA
MALAWI

IMBABWE

MOZAMBIQUE

MADAGASCAR

TH
CA

Singapore
2105

MALAYSIA
BRUNEI

INDONESIA
Bandung
974
Surabaya

PAPUA
NEW
GUINEA

1283

WESTERN SAMOA

FIJI

AUSTRALIA

NEW
ZEALAND

WASTE

WASTE THROWN OUT
EACH DAY PER PERSON
1985 or latest year available
1 kg = 2.2 lbs

1.75 kgs
.75 kg

data not available

TOTAL MUNICIPAL WASTE
GENERATED EACH DAY
where available, mid-1980s
1 tonne = .98 ton

over 5000 tonnes

1000 – 5000 tonnes

under 1000 tonnes

For sewage see Map 16; for industrial waste
see Map 25; for toxic waste see Map 27.

45

ICELAND

CANADA

FINLAND

NORWAY

SWEDEN

IRELAND

UNITED KINGDOM

DENMARK · **R. Odense**

USSR

R. Maas

R. Rhine

EAST GERMANY

POLAND

R. Thames

BEL

NETH

LUX

R. Meuse

CZECHOSLOVAKIA

R. Seine

Espierre R.

WEST GERMANY

AUSTRIA

HUNG

R. Danube

ROMAN

FRANCE

SWITZ

UNITED STATES OF AMERICA

ITALY

YUGOSLAVIA

BULG

R. Mino

R. Rhône

BERMUDA

PORTUGAL

SPAIN

ALBANIA

GREECE

GIBRALTAR (Br)

R. Tejo

R. Ebro

MEXICO

R. Lerma

MOROCCO

TUNISIA

LIBY

Atoyac R.

CUBA

BAHAMAS

ALGERIA

GUATEMALA

BELIZE

HONDURAS

EL SALVADOR

NICARAGUA

COSTA RICA

PANAMA

HAITI

JAMAICA

DOMINICAN REPUBLIC

PUERTO RICO (US)

GUADELOUPE (Fr)

DOMINICA

MARTINIQUE (Fr)

BARBADOS

TRINIDAD & TOBAGO

ATLANTIC OCEAN

CAPE VERDE

WESTERN SAHARA

MAURITANIA

MALI

NIGER

CH

SENEGAL

GAMBIA

GUINEA-BISSAU

GUINEA

SIERRA LEONE

LIBERIA

IVORY COAST

GHANA

BURKINA

BENN

TOGO

NIGERIA

CAMEROON

EQUATORIAL GUINEA

SAO TOME & PRINCIPE

GABON

CONGO

PACIFIC OCEAN

Cauca Juanchito R.

VENEZUELA

GUYANA

SURINAME

FRENCH GUIANA (Fr)

COLOMBIA

ECUADOR

PERU

BRAZIL

BOLIVIA

PARAGUAY

Paraiba do Sul-Barra Mansa R.

ANGO

NAMIB

CHILE

ARGENTINA

URUGUA

FALKLAND ISLANDS (Br)

SEWAGE

PROPORTION OF PEOPLE IN CITIES WITHOUT ADEQUATE SANITARY FACILITIES
mid-1980s averages

- 75%
- 50%
- 25%
- 10%

data not available

SEWAGE POLLUTION OF RIVERS

grossly polluted

severely polluted

For drinking water safety see Map 6; for waste disposal see Map 15; for beach pollution see Map 32.

86				
	23	22	17	17
Iceland	Portugal	Norway	Ireland	Greece

Proportion of untreated sewage dumped at sea
mid-1980s percentages

OCEAN DUMPING

46

Data compiled by Lesley Downing   Main sources: Monitoring and Assessment Research Centre (1987); UNEP(1989);WHO *World Health Statistics Annual (1986)*.

The growth of city populations is overwhelming existing systems for safe disposal of sewage. Many urban rivers have become virtual open sewers.

UNION OF SOVIET SOCIALIST REPUBLICS

MONGOLIA

CHINA

TURKEY

CYPRUS
LEBANON
ISRAEL
SYRIA
JOR
IRAQ
IRAN
AFGHANISTAN
PAKISTAN

KUWAIT
BAHRAIN
QATAR
U.A.E.
SAUDI ARABIA
OMAN
N. S. YEMEN
YEMEN
DJIBOUTI

EGYPT

SUDAN

ETHIOPIA

UGANDA
KENYA
TANZANIA
COMOROS
MALAWI
ZIMBABWE
MOZAMBIQUE
MADAGASCAR

Yamuna R.

Sabarmati R.

Narmada R.

INDIA

Subernarekha R.

NEPAL
BHUTAN
BANGLADESH
MYANMAR
LAOS
THAILAND
CAM
VIETNAM

Kelani R.
SRI LANKA

MALDIVES

Klang R.
MALAYSIA
SINGAPORE
BRUNEI

N KOREA
S KOREA
JAPAN
Yodo R.

TAIWAN

PACIFIC
OCEAN

INDONESIA

PAPUA
NEW
GUINEA

WESTERN SAMOA
FIJI

AUSTRALIA

NEW
ZEALAND

Disposal of sewage sludge, after treatment
mid-1980s percentages

Ireland: 46 / 17 / 29 / 8
Japan: 50 / 16 / 34
Netherlands: 6 / 27 / 4 / 62 / 1
Spain: 29 / 10 / 61
UK: 29 / 10 / 4 / 45 / 12
USA: 4 / 15 / 27 / 42 / 12
New York City: 37 / 25 / 38
USSR: 75 / 25

- ocean dumping
- landfill
- incineration
- recycling
- unknown

THE END OF THE MATTER?

AIR QUALITY

CITIES WITH AIR QUALITY
PROBLEMS
Annual averages *mid-1980s*
Known pollution is greatest from
high levels of

sulphur dioxide

nitrogen oxides

both

*High level exceeds international safe
health guidelines*

medium levels of:

sulphur dioxide

nitrogen oxides

both

*Most sulphur dioxide comes from burning
fossil fuels; most nitrogen oxides come
from cars.*

For acid rain see Map 24; for fossil fuel
pollution see Map 23.

48

Data compiled by Claire Holman Main sources: GEMS (1988); World Resources Institute (1988); OECD (1989).

In many cities, just breathing is a health hazard.

CHOKING

PROPORTION OF AIR POLLUTION CAUSED BY CARS IN OECD COUNTRIES *late 1980s* percentages

75%

48%

13%

3%

carbon monoxide

nitrogen oxides

dirt and dust

sulphur oxides

UNION OF SOVIET SOCIALIST REPUBLICS

TURKEY

CYPRUS
SYRIA IRAQ
LEB
ISRAEL

Tel Aviv

EGYPT

SAUDI ARABIA

SUDAN

N S YEMEN
YEMEN

DJIBOUTI

IRAN

KUWAIT
BAHRAIN
QATAR
U A E
OMAN

AFGHANISTAN

PAKISTAN

Tehran

Delhi

Calcutta

INDIA

NEPAL BHUTAN

B
DESH

MYANMAR

LAOS
THAI

CAM

VIETNAM

SRI LANKA

MALDIVES

CHINA

Shenyang

Beijing

Xian

Guangzhou

Shanghai

Hong Kong

N KOREA

Seoul

JAPAN

Tokyo

Osaka

TAIWAN

Manila

PHILIPPINES

BRUNEI
W

MALAYSIA
SINGAPORE

INDONESIA

PAPUA
NEW
GUINEA

PACIFIC
OCEAN

AUSTRALIA

WESTERN SAMOA

FIJI

Sydney

Melbourne

NEW
ZEALAND

Oslo

Helsinki

Glasgow

Copenhagen

Stockholm

Amsterdam

Warsaw

Dublin

Frankfurt

London

Antwerp

Prague

Paris

Zürich

Toulouse

Milan

Zagreb

Madrid

Rome

sbon

Athens

Cairo

Kuwait

Delhi

Calcutta

Bombay

Shenyang

Beijing

Xian

Shanghai

Guangzhou

Tokyo

Osaka

Hong Kong

Bangkok

Manila

Kuala Lumpur

Jakarta

Sydney

Melbourne

Christchurch

ILL WIND

DIRT AND DUST LEVELS IN CITIES
1980s latest year available
annual average

high
*level exceeds international
safe health guidelines*

medium

low

49

Copyright © Swanston Publishing Limited

GREENLAND
(Den)

ICELAND

NORWAY
SWEDEN
DENMARK
UNITED
KINGDOM
IRELAND
NETH
BEL
GER
W GER
PO
AUS
FRANCE
YUGOS
ITALY
PORTUGAL   SPAIN

CANADA

UNITED STATES
OF AMERICA

ATLANTIC
OCEAN

TUNISIA
MOROCCO
ALGERIA
LIBY
BERMUDA
WESTERN SAHARA

MEXICO

BAHAMAS

CUBA
HAITI
DOMINICAN REPUBLIC
PUERTO RICO (US)
BELIZE
HONDURAS   JAMAICA
GUATEMALA
EL SALVADOR   GUADELOUPE (Fr)
NICARAGUA   DOMINICA
MARTINIQUE (Fr)
BARBADOS
COSTA RICA   TRINIDAD & TOBAGO
PANAMA

MAURITANIA
MALI
NIGER
CAPE VERDE
SENEGAL
GAMBIA
CH
GUINEA-BISSAU
GUINEA
BURKINA
BENIN
NIGERIA
SIERRA LEONE   IVORY
COAST   GHANA
LIBERIA   TOGO
CAMEROON

VENEZUELA   GUYANA
SURINAME
FRENCH GUIANA (Fr)
COLOMBIA

ECUADOR

PERU

BRAZIL

EQUATORIAL GUINEA
SAO TOME & PRINCIPE   GABON
CONGO

ATLANTIC
OCEAN

ANG

BOLIVIA

PARAGUAY

PACIFIC
OCEAN

NAMIBI

CHILE

URUGUAY

ARGENTINA

ENERGY BUDGETS

ANNUAL ENERGY CONSUMPTION
PER PERSON
1987 gigajoules

200
100
50
15

data not available

World average : 66; extremes: Qatar 642;
Comoros 2

FALKLAND ISLANDS (Br)

Data compiled by Lisa Greber   Main sources: IEA (1989); UN *Energy Statistics Yearbook* (1989).

There is neither social nor environmental balance in today's global energy budget.

POWER SHARES
Sources of world energy 1987

nuclear 5

hydro 6

oil 32

fuelwood 14

%

coal 26

gas 17

POWER HUNGRY

USA & Canada 26%

Europe 23%

USSR 18%

China 8%

Japan 5%

Central America 1%

Africa 4%

South America 4%

Middle East 2%

India 3%

Rest of Asia 5%

Oceania 1%

shares of world energy consumption *1987*

51

Copyright © Swanston Publishing Limited

CANADA

UNITED STATES
OF AMERICA

MEXICO

BERMUDA

BAHAMAS

CUBA

HAITI
DOMINICAN REPUBLIC
PUERTO RICO (US)

JAMAICA

GUATEMALA
EL SALVADOR
BELIZE
HONDURAS
NICARAGUA
COSTA RICA
PANAMA

GUADELOUPE (Fr)
DOMINICA
MARTINIQUE (Fr)
BARBADOS
TRINIDAD & TOBAGO

VENEZUELA
COLOMBIA
ECUADOR
PERU

GUYANA
SURINAME
FRENCH GUIANA (Fr)

BRAZIL

BOLIVIA
PARAGUAY

CHILE
ARGENTINA
URUGUAY

FALKLAND ISLANDS (Br)

PACIFIC
OCEAN

ATLANTIC
OCEAN

ICELAND

NORWAY
SWEDEN
FINLAND

UNITED
KINGDOM
IRELAND
DENMARK

USSR

NETH
W.GER
BEL
LUX
EAST
GERMANY
POLAND

FRANCE
CZECHOSLOVAKIA

SWITZ
AUSTRIA
HUNGARY
ROMA

PORTUGAL
SPAIN
ITALY
YUGOSLAVIA
BU

ALBANIA
GREE

GIBRALTAR (Br)

MOROCCO
TUNISIA

WESTERN SAHARA
ALGERIA
LIB

MAURITANIA
MALI
NIGER

CAPE VERDE
SENEGAL
GAMBIA
GUINEA BISSAU
GUINEA
SIERRA LEONE
LIBERIA
IVORY
COAST
GHANA
BURKINA
BENIN
NIGERIA

CAMEROON
GABON
CONGO
ANG
NAMI

THE NUCLEAR FAMILY

NUCLEAR POWER PLANTS
1989

more than 25 in operation

10-25 in operation

less than 10 in operation

plants planned or under
construction

research reactors or other
nuclear facilities

other countries

THE NUCLEAR FUEL CYCLE *1989*

uranium mining

uranium refining plant

uranium enrichment plant

nuclear fuel fabrication
plant

spent fuel reprocessing
plant

For military nuclear activities see Map 30.

Data compiled by Lisa Greber   Main sources: International Atomic Energy Agency (1989); *Nuclear News* (August 1989).

There are more than 400 nuclear power plants operating in 26 countries. But an even greater number of states participate in the supply and support of the nuclear industry.

UNION OF SOVIET SOCIALIST REPUBLICS

MONGOLIA

CHINA

N KOREA
S KOREA
JAPAN

TURKEY
CYPRUS
LEBANON
SYRIA
ISRAEL JOR
IRAQ
IRAN
AFGHANISTAN
EGYPT
KUWAIT
BAHRAIN
QATAR
UAE
SAUDI ARABIA
OMAN
PAKISTAN
NEPAL
BHUTAN
B
DESH
INDIA
MYANMAR
LAOS
THAILAND
CAM
VIETNAM
TAIWAN
PACIFIC OCEAN
PHILIPPINES

N
YEMEN
S YEMEN
DJIBOUTI
ETHIOPIA
SOMALIA
UGANDA
KENYA
TANZANIA
SEYCHELLES
COMOROS
MALAWI
ZIMBABWE
MOZAMBIQUE
MADAGASCAR

INDIAN OCEAN

BRUNEI
MALAYSIA
SINGAPORE
INDONESIA
PAPUA NEW GUINEA

WESTERN SAMOA
FIJI

AUSTRALIA

NEW ZEALAND

NUCLEAR GENERATION

Sources of electricity generated top 10 countries
mid-1980s percentages

| nuclear power | | other |

	France	Belgium	Hungary	S.Korea	Switzerland	Bulgaria	Spain	Finland	W.Germany	Czech
other						30	34			
			51	53		63	64	64	64	66	73
nuclear	70	66	49	47	37	36	36	36	34	27

GREENLAND
(Den)

ICELAND

NORWAY

SWEDEN

CANADA

DENMARK

UNITED
KINGDOM

IRELAND

NETH
BEL

POLA

E
GER

W GER

CZECH

AUS

HUN

FRANCE

S

ITALY

YUGOSL

UNITED STATES
OF AMERICA

PORTUGAL   SPAIN

GH

ATLANTIC
OCEAN

BERMUDA

MOROCCO

TUNISIA

ALGERIA

LIBYA

MEXICO

BAHAMAS

CUBA

HAITI

DOMINICAN REPUBLIC
PUERTO RICO (US)

JAMAICA

BELIZE
HONDURAS

GUATEMALA
EL SALVADOR

NICARAGUA

COSTA RICA

PANAMA

GUADELOUPE (Fr)

DOMINICA

MARTINIQUE (Fr)

BARBADOS

TRINIDAD & TOBAGO

WESTERN SAHARA

MAURITANIA

MALI

NIGER

CHAD

CAPE VERDE

SENEGAL

GAMBIA

GUINEA-BISSAU

BURKINA

GUINEA

SIERRA LEONE

LIBERIA

IVORY
COAST

GHANA

TOGO

BENIN

NIGERIA

**Kainji dam
42,000 people**

CA

VENEZUELA

GUYANA

SURINAME

FRENCH GUIANA (Fr)

COLOMBIA

**Akosombo dam
78,000 people**

CAMEROON

EQUATORIAL GUINEA

SAO TOME & PRINCIPE

GABON

CONGO

PACIFIC
OCEAN

ECUADOR

B R A Z I L

**Tucurui dam
20-30,000 people**

ANGOL

PERU

**Sobradinho dam
60,000 people**

**Itaparica dam
40,000 people**

BOLIVIA

NAMIBIA

PARAGUAY

**Itaipu dam
50,000 people**

CHILE

ARGENTINA

URUGUAY

**Yacreta dam
45,000 people**

64	27	21	20	12	9	7	2
Canada	India	Spain	China	Japan	USA	S Korea	UK

Proportion of electricity generated by hydro power
selected countries *1987* percentages

FALKLAND ISLANDS (Br)

DAM DEPENDENCE

DAMMING THE AMAZON

VENEZUELA

GUYANA

SURINAME

FRENCH
GUIANA (Fr)

COLOMBIA

R. Amazon

**Balbina
dam**

**Tucurui
dam**

25 NEW DAMS PLANNED

**Samuel
dam**

PERU

BOLIVIA

54

Data compiled by Constance E Hunt   Main sources: International Commission on Large Dams (1984); Mermel (1989); Simons (1989);

Hydro power is a cheap and renewable
energy source, but dams often carry a
high social and environmental price tag.

UNION OF SOVIET SOCIALIST REPUBLICS

MONGOLIA

N.KOREA

S.KOREA

JAPAN

CHINA

TAIWAN

*PACIFIC
OCEAN*

TURKEY

Keban dam
30,000 people

CYPRUS
LEBANON
ISRAEL JOR
SYRIA
IRAQ
IRAN
AFGHANISTAN
PAKISTAN
KUWAIT
BAHRAIN
QATAR
U.A.E.
SAUDI ARABIA
OMAN
N. S.YEMEN
YEMEN

EGYPT

Aswan dam
120,000 people

NEPAL BHUTAN

INDIA

B
DESH

MYANMAR

Three Gorges dam
1 million people

Sardar Sarovar dam
70,000 people

THAILAND

LAOS

CAM VIETNAM

PHILIPPINES

SUDAN

ETHIOPIA

SOMALIA

SRI LANKA

MALDIVES

BRUNEI

MALAYSIA

SINGAPORE

UGANDA
KENYA

BURUNDI
TANZANIA

SEYCHELLES

INDIAN OCEAN

INDONESIA

PAPUA
NEW
GUINEA

COMOROS

ZAMBIA
MALAWI
MOZAMBIQUE

MADAGASCAR

WESTERN SAMOA

FIJI

ZIMBABWE

Cabora Bassa dam
25,000 people

Kariba dam
57,000 people

JTH
CA

AUSTRALIA

NEW
ZEALAND

HYDRO POWER

NUMBER OF LARGE DAMS
Dams over 15 metres high *mid-1980s*

- 1000
- 500
- 250
- 50

data not
available

**DAMS WITH EXCEPTIONAL IMPACT
ON THE ENVIRONMENT**

dam known to have forced
relocation of more than
10,000 people *since early
1970s*

planned dam which would
force major relocation of
people

DAMMED ELECTRICITY

over 90% of electricity
generated by hydro power

Extreme: China 18,595 dams

GREENLAND
(Den)

ICELAND

C A N A D A

NORWAY
SWEDEN

DENMARK

UNITED
KINGDOM
IRELAND
NETH
BEL
E GER
POR
W GER
CZECH
AUS
H
UNITED STATES
OF AMERICA

FRANCE
YUGOS
ITALY

PORTUGAL
SPAIN

BERMUDA

A T L A N T I C
O C E A N

TUNISIA

MOROCCO
ALGERIA
LIBY

BAHAMAS

WESTERN SAHARA

CUBA
HAITI
DOMINICAN REPUBLIC
PUERTO RICO (US)

MAURITANIA
MALI
NIGER

BELIZE
GUATEMALA
HONDURAS
JAMAICA
EL SALVADOR
NICARAGUA
DOMINICA
MARTINIQUE (Fr)
BARBADOS
TRINIDAD & TOBAGO
GUADELOUPE (Fr)

MEXICO

CAPE VERDE
SENEGAL
GAMBIA
GUINEA-BISSAU
GUINEA
SIERRA LEONE
LIBERIA
BURKINA
IVORY
COAST
GHANA
TOGO
BENIN
NIGERIA
C
CAMEROON

COSTA RICA
PANAMA
VENEZUELA
GUYANA
SURINAME
FRENCH GUIANA (Fr)
COLOMBIA

ECUADOR

EQUATORIAL GUINEA
SAO TOME & PRINCIPE
GABON
CONGO

PERU

B R A Z I L

ANGO

BOLIVIA

A T L A N T I C
O C E A N

NAMIBI

PARAGUAY

CHILE

ARGENTINA

FALKLAND ISLANDS (Br)

0.5	1.5	1.5	3.0	3.0	3.0	4.0	4.5	5.0	
Bangladesh	Sudan, Bara	Tanzania	Africa, Sahel	Nepal, Tinan	Kenya	Niger	Burkina	India, Chamoli	

Hours per day that women spend
collecting firewood
early 1980s

THE WALK TO WOOD

Data compiled by Thomas E Downing   Main sources: Agarwal (1986); FAO (1981); UN Statistical Office (1987).

Firewood, the primary source of energy
for many people in the world, is
increasingly short in supply.

UNION OF SOVIET SOCIALIST REPUBLICS

MONGOLIA

CHINA

N KOREA

S KOREA

JAPAN

PACIFIC
OCEAN

TAIWAN

TURKEY

CYPRUS
LEBANON
ISRAEL JOR
SYRIA

IRAQ

IRAN

AFGHANISTAN

PAKISTAN

KUWAIT

BAHRAIN

QATAR
U.A.E

EGYPT

SAUDI ARABIA

OMAN

N YEMEN S YEMEN

DJIBOUTI

SUDAN

ETHIOPIA

SOMALIA

KENYA

SEYCHELLES

COMOROS

MADAGASCAR

MALAWI

ZIMBABWE

MOZAMBIQUE

SOUTH
AFRICA

NEPAL

BHUTAN

B
DESH

INDIA

MYANMAR

SRI LANKA

MALDIVES

LAOS

THAILAND

CAM

VIETNAM

PHILIPPINES

BRUNEI

MALAYSIA

SINGAPORE

INDONESIA

PAPUA
NEW
GUINEA

AUSTRALIA

NEW
ZEALAND

WESTERN SAMOA

FIJI

FIREWOOD

PROPORTION OF ENERGY
SUPPLIED BY FUELWOOD
AND CHARCOAL
1985 percentages

more than 90%

60%

30%

5%

data not available

SPREADING SCARCITY
Availability of fuelwood
early 1980s

scarcity already acute

current supply falls short
of demand

crisis predicted

For energy use see Map 18.

GREENLAND
(Den)

ICELAND

NORWAY

SWEDEN

DENMARK

CANADA

**Exxon
Valdez**

HAWAII

Hawaiian Patriot

UNITED STATES
OF AMERICA

IRELAND

UNITED
KINGDOM

NETH
BEL

E
GER

POL

CZECH
W GER AUS

YUGOS

FRANCE

**Torrey Canyon
Amoco Cadiz
Texaco Denmark**

Urquiola

PORTUGAL

SPAIN

ITALY

MEXICO

BERMUDA

BAHAMAS

CUBA

HAITI

BELIZE

JAMAICA

DOMINICAN REPUBLIC
PUERTO RICO (US)

HONDURAS

GUATEMALA
EL SALVADOR

GUADELOUPE (Fr)

DOMINICA

MARTINIQUE (Fr)

NICARAGUA

**Atlantic Express/
Aegean Captain**

BARBADOS

COSTA RICA

PANAMA

TRINIDAD
TOBAGO

VENEZUELA

GUYANA

SURINAME

FRENCH GUIANA (Fr)

COLOMBIA

ECUADOR

PERU

*ATLANTIC
OCEAN*

MOROCCO

ALGERIA

LIBY

WESTERN SAHARA

TUNISI

MAURITANIA

MALI

NIGER

CHA

CAPE VERDE

SENEGAL

GAMBIA

GUINEA-BISSAU

GUINEA

SIERRA LEONE

LIBERIA

IVORY
COAST

GHANA

TOGO

BENIN

NIGERIA

CA

CAMEROON

EQUATORIAL GUINEA

SAO TOME & PRINCIPE

GABON

CONGO

*PACIFIC
OCEAN*

B R A Z I L

BOLIVIA

PARAGUAY

CHILE

URUGUAY

ARGENTINA

*ATLANTIC
OCEAN*

NAMIBIA

**Castillo de
Belver**

ANGO

FALKLAND ISLANDS (Br)

OILY BUSINESS

Rating of oil
companies'
accident records

best

Ashland

Shell
Exxon
Chevron/Gulf

Mobil
Marathon
Sun

Texaco/Getty
BP
Arco
Conoco

Phillips

Amerada Hess

worst

OIL POLLUTION

TANKER ACCIDENTS CAUSING
SEVERE OCEAN OIL POLLUTION
1967-89 tonnes

more than 100,000

30,000-100,000

1000-30,000

oil rig blowouts

THE TOP OIL CONSUMERS
1987

countries which together
consume two-thirds of the
world's oil

For other industrial accidents see Map 26.

58

Data compiled by Dominic Golding   Main sources: Couper (1983); ITOPF (1983); Levy (1984); McKenzie (1989); NAS (1985); OECD *Environmental Data Compendium* (1989);
Tanker Advisory Center (1989); UNEP *Environmental Data Report* (1989).

Dependence on oil is a defining feature of modern industrial economies, as is the pollution it leaves in its wake.

OCEANS OF OIL
Causes of ocean oil pollution mid-1980s

%

offshore production 2

other shipping sources
12

natural sources
8

atmospheric releases
9

tanker accidents
12

municipal and industrial runoff
36

routine tanker discharges
21

UNION OF SOVIET SOCIALIST REPUBLICS

TURKEY

SYRIA
LEBANON
ISRAEL JOR
IRAQ
IRAN
AFGHANISTAN
CHINA
N KOREA
S KOREA
JAPAN

GYPT
KUWAIT
BAHRAIN
QATAR
U.A.E
OMAN
PAKISTAN
NEPAL
BHUTAN
B
DESH
MYANMAR
LAOS
TAIWAN

SAUDI ARABIA
Sea Star
INDIA
SRI LANKA
THAILAND
CAM
VIETNAM

UDAN
N
S YEMEN
YEMEN
DJIBOUTI

ETHIOPIA
SOMALIA
MALDIVES
MALAYSIA
SINGAPORE
BRUNEI

UGANDA
KENYA

SEYCHELLES
INDONESIA
PAPUA NEW GUINEA

TANZANIA

COMOROS
INDIAN OCEAN

MALAWI

MBABWE
MADAGASCAR

MOZAMBIQUE

PACIFIC OCEAN

WESTERN SAMOA
FIJI

AUSTRALIA

NEW ZEALAND

CHRONIC OIL TRAILS

Oil pollution from routine shipping operations

ICELAND

NORWAY

FINLAND

SWEDEN

IRELAND

DENMARK

U S S R

UNITED
KINGDOM

NETH

EAST
GERMANY

POLAND

BEL

WEST
GERMANY

CZECHOSLOVAKIA

LUX

FRANCE

SWITZ

AUSTRIA

HUNGARY

ROM

ITALY

YUGOSLAVIA

PORTUGAL

SPAIN

ALBANIA

GREE

GIBRALTAR (Br)

CANADA

UNITED STATES
OF AMERICA

BERMUDA

MEXICO

BAHAMAS

CUBA

TUNISIA

HAITI

DOMINICAN REPUBLIC

PUERTO RICO (US)

MOROCCO

ALGERIA

LIB

BELIZE

JAMAICA

GUATEMALA

HONDURAS

GUADELOUPE (Fr)

WESTERN SAHARA

DOMINICA

EL SALVADOR

MARTINIQUE (Fr)

NICARAGUA

BARBADOS

MAURITANIA

MALI

NIGER

COSTA RICA

TRINIDAD & TOBAGO

CAPE VERDE

SENEGAL

PANAMA

VENEZUELA

GUYANA

GAMBIA

BURKINA

C

SURINAME

GUINEA-BISSAU

NIGERIA

COLOMBIA

FRENCH GUIANA (Fr)

GUINEA

SIERRA LEONE

IVORY
COAST

GHANA

BENIN

ECUADOR

LIBERIA

TOGO

CAMEROON

PERU

EQUATORIAL GUINEA

SAO TOME & PRINCIPE

GABON

B R A Z I L

CONGO

ANG

BOLIVIA

PARAGUAY

FOSSIL FUEL POLLUTION	

CARBON DIOXIDE PRODUCED BY
BURNING OIL, COAL AND GAS
per person per year
1987 tonnes

CHILE

15

10

URUGUAY

5

ARGENTINA

1

NAMI

data not available

World average 3.6 tonnes per person
per year.

FALKLAND ISLANDS (Br)

For global warming see Map 1; for air
quality see Map 17; for acid rain see
Map 24.

60

Data compiled by Claire Holman   Main sources: Eliasson et.al. (1988); GEMS (1988); Oak Ridge National Laboratory (1988).

There is now 25 per cent more carbon dioxide in the atmosphere than there was at the beginning of the Industrial Revolution. It is the major cause of global warming.

UNION OF SOVIET SOCIALIST REPUBLICS

MONGOLIA

N KOREA

S KOREA

JAPAN

TURKEY

CYPRUS
LEBANON
ISRAEL
SYRIA
JORDAN
IRAQ
IRAN
AFGHANISTAN
CHINA

GYPT
KUWAIT
BAHRAIN
QATAR
UAE
SAUDI ARABIA
OMAN
PAKISTAN
NEPAL
BHUTAN
INDIA
B
DESH
MYANMAR
LAOS
HONG KONG (Br)
TAIWAN

UDAN
N
YEMEN
S YEMEN
DJIBOUTI
THAILAND
CAM
VIETNAM
PHILIPPINES

ETHIOPIA
SOMALIA

UGANDA
KENYA
MALDIVES
SRI LANKA
BRUNEI
MALAYSIA
SINGAPORE

TANZANIA
SEYCHELLES
INDONESIA
PAPUA NEW GUINEA

COMOROS

MALAWI

MBABWE
MOZAMBIQUE
MADAGASCAR
AUSTRALIA

WESTERN SAMOA

FIJI

FUELLING THE PROBLEM

CANADA

U S A

UNITED KINGDOM

E GER
POLAND

W GER
CZECH

FRANCE

ITALY

SPAIN

USSR

CHINA

JAPAN

NEW ZEALAND

HAZARDOUS GASES RELEASED BY BURNING FOSSIL FUELS
Top 12 producers *mid-1980s* tonnes

Nitrogen oxides	over 10,000	under 5000	Sulphur dioxide	over 10,000	under 5000

Copyright © Swanston Publishing Limited

ICELAND

NORWAY
SWEDEN
FINLAND

DENMARK
IRELAND
UNITED KINGDOM
EAST GERMANY
POLAND
FRANCE
PORTUGAL
SPAIN
GIBRALTAR (Br)
ALBANIA

C A N A D A

UNITED STATES OF AMERICA

BERMUDA

MEXICO
BAHAMAS
CUBA
BELIZE
HAITI
DOMINICAN REPUBLIC
PUERTO RICO (US)
GUATEMALA
HONDURAS
JAMAICA
EL SALVADOR
GUADELOUPE (Fr)
DOMINICA
NICARAGUA
MARTINIQUE (Fr)
BARBADOS
COSTA RICA
TRINIDAD & TOBAGO
PANAMA
VENEZUELA
GUYANA
SURINAME
COLOMBIA
FRENCH GUIANA (Fr)

ECUADOR
PERU
B R A Z I L
BOLIVIA
PARAGUAY

PACIFIC OCEAN

CHILE
URUGUAY
ARGENTINA

FALKLAND ISLANDS (Br)

MOROCCO
TUNISIA
ALGERIA
LIB
WESTERN SAHARA
MAURITANIA
MALI
NIGER
CAPE VERDE
SENEGAL
GAMBIA
GUINEA-BISSAU
GUINEA
BURKINA
BENIN
NIGERIA
SIERRA LEONE
IVORY COAST
GHANA
TOGO
LIBERIA
CAMEROON
EQUATORIAL GUINEA
SAO TOME & PRINCIPE
GABON
CONGO

ATLANTIC OCEAN

ANG
NAMIE

ACID RAIN

LEVELS OF ACID RAIN POLLUTION
mid-1980s

The main components of acid rain are sulphur dioxide and nitrogen oxides. These are released by burning oil, coal and gas.

high
very high
extremely high
early signs of acid rain pollution

For air quality see Map 17; for fossil fuel pollution see Map 23.

62

Data compiled by Friends of the Earth/Mike Birkin   Main sources: Goldsmith & Hildyard eds. (1988); UNEP, *Forest Damage & Air Pollution* (1989); McCormick (1989); World Resources Institute (1988).

Acid rain is the fallout of industrial and fossil-fuel dependent economies. After falling on Europe for more than 100 years it is now becoming a global phenomenon.

UNION OF SOVIET SOCIALIST REPUBLICS

MONGOLIA

CHINA

N KOREA

S KOREA

JAPAN

TURKEY

CYPRUS
LEBANON
ISRAEL
JOR
IRAQ
SYRIA
IRAN
AFGHANISTAN
KUWAIT
BAHRAIN
QATAR
UAE
OMAN
SAUDI ARABIA
PAKISTAN
NEPAL
BHUTAN
INDIA
B
DESH
MYANMAR
LAOS
THAILAND
CAM
VIETNAM
TAIWAN

PACIFIC
OCEAN

PHILIPPINES

EGYPT
N YEMEN
S YEMEN
DJIBOUTI
SUDAN
ETHIOPIA
SOMALIA
SRI LANKA
MALDIVES

BRUNEI
MALAYSIA
SINGAPORE
INDONESIA

UGANDA
KENYA
RE
TANZANIA
SEYCHELLES

INDIAN OCEAN

PAPUA
NEW
GUINEA

BIA
ZIMBABWE
MOZAMBIQUE
MALAWI
TH
CA

DEAD WOOD

NORWAY
SWEDEN
FINLAND
Estonia
DENMARK
Lithuania
IRELAND
UNITED
KINGDOM
NETH
BEL
LUX
WEST
GERMANY
EAST
GERMANY
POLAND
USSR
CZECHOSLOVAKIA
SWITZ
AUSTRIA
HUNGARY
ROMANIA
FRANCE
ITALY
Tuscany
YUGOSLAVIA
BULGARIA
PORTUGAL
SPAIN
ALBANIA
GREECE
GIBRALTAR (Br)

WESTERN SAMOA
FIJI

AUSTRALIA

NEW
ZEALAND

FORESTS DAMAGED BY ACID RAIN POLLUTION
1988 percentages

- 60%
- 50%
- 40%
- 30%
- 20%

data not available

Extremes: Czechoslovakia 70.5% – Portugal 3.5%

ICELAND

FINLAND

NORWAY SWEDEN

Gruinard
Island

North
Sea

DENMARK

Baltic
Sea

USSR

Sellafield

Teesside

IRELAND

UNITED
KINGDOM

Merseyside

R. Thames

Ruhr
region

NETH

EAST
GERMANY

BEL

WEST
GERMANY

R. Vistula

POLAND

Silesia
Krakow

CZECH.

Meuse
Valley

LUX

Bohemia

HUNG

FRANCE

SWITZ

Seveso

AUSTRIA

R. Danube

ROMAN

R. Dunau

ITALY

YUGOSLAVIA

BUL

PORTUGAL

SPAIN

Mediterranean
Sea

ALBANIA

GREECE

GIBRALTAR (Br)

C A N A D A

Hanford

Sudbury

UNITED STATES
OF AMERICA

Great
Lakes

Love Canal

South
Chicago

Contra Costa
County

Rocky
Flats

Times
Beach

Meadowlands

Institute

Mississippi R.

BERMUDA

MEXICO

BAHAMAS

A T L A N T I C
O C E A N

MOROCCO

TUNISIA

ALGERIA

LIBYA

Mexico City

CUBA

HAITI

JAMAICA

DOMINICAN REPUBLIC

PUERTO RICO (US)

WESTERN SAHARA

BELIZE

GUATEMALA

HONDURAS

EL SALVADOR

NICARAGUA

COSTA RICA

PANAMA

GUADELOUPE (Fr)

DOMINICA

MARTINIQUE (Fr)

BARBADOS

TRINIDAD & TOBAGO

VENEZUELA

GUYANA

SURINAME

FRENCH GUIANA (Fr)

MAURITANIA

MALI

NIGER

CHA

CAPE VERDE

SENEGAL

GAMBIA

GUINEA-BISSAU

GUINEA

SIERRA LEONE

LIBERIA

IVORY
COAST

BURKINA

GHANA

TOGO

BENIN

NIGERIA

CAMEROON

COLOMBIA

ECUADOR

EQUATORIAL GUINEA

SAO TOME & PRINCIPE

GABON

CONGO

PERU

B R A Z I L

ANG

BOLIVIA

Cubatao

NAMIB

PARAGUAY

CHILE

URUGUAY

ARGENTINA

FALKLAND ISLANDS (Br)

Bar chart — Industrial waste dumped at sea mid-1980s '000 tonnes

Country	Value
UK	9904
France	9508
W Germany	6945
Hong Kong	4490
USA	4034
Belgium	3143
Ireland	3090
Italy	1000

Industrial waste dumped at sea
mid-1980s '000 tonnes

SULLIED SEAS

INDUSTRIAL WASTE

ANNUAL INDUSTRIAL PRODUCTION
OF HAZARDOUS WASTE
1988 tonnes

1 million

500,000

100,000

data not available/other

BLIGHTED ZONES

extreme level of chronic
industrial pollution

DEAD ZONES

uninhabitable as result of
industrial or military/
industrial activities

For export of hazardous waste see Map 27;
for catastrophic industrial accidents see
Map 26.

Data compiled by Joni Seager   Main sources: National Wildlife Federation *The Toxic 500 1987* (1989); UNEP *Environmental Data Report* (1989).

Chronic pollution and a worldwide trail of hazardous waste are hallmarks of the industrial age.

Kola Peninsula

UNION OF SOVIET SOCIALIST REPUBLICS

Sverdlovsk

ernobyl   Kharkov   Kyshtym

MONGOLIA

Songhua R.

Liao He   Ishikari R.

Beijing   JAPAN

Caspian Sea   N KOREA   Tokyo

TURKEY   C H I N A   S KOREA   Yokkaichi

CYPRUS   SYRIA   AFGHANISTAN
LEBANON   JOR
ISRAEL   IRAQ   IRAN   PACIFIC
EGYPT   KUWAIT   PAKISTAN   OCEAN
BAHRAIN
QATAR   NEPAL   BHUTAN
UAE   TAIWAN

SAUDI ARABIA   OMAN   Bhopal   B
DESH
MYANMAR   HONG KONG (Br)

N   S YEMEN   I N D I A
YEMEN   West
DJIBOUTI   Bombay   LAOS

SUDAN   THAILAND   CAM   VIETNAM   PHILIPPINES

ETHIOPIA   Bikini
Island

SRI LANKA   BRUNEI
Runit
KENYA   MALDIVES   SINGAPORE   M A L A Y S I A   Island

SEYCHELLES

COMOROS   I N D O N E S I A   PAPUA
NEW
TANZANIA   GUINEA

MALAWI   WESTERN SAMOA

MADAGASCAR   FIJI

MOZAMBIQUE   A U S T R A L I A

ZIMBABWE

NEW
ZEALAND

THE CORPORATE WAY

Toxins released from US industrial plant (parent companies) *1987*

- toxic chemicals, thousand tonnes
- known cancer-causing chemicals, tonnes

Company	Value
Aluminum Co. of America	452
National Steel	349
Du Pont de Nemours	154
British Petroleum	152
Monsanto	108
Pfizer	4639
Eastman Kodak	4538
Du Pont de Nemours	4391
General Electric	3775
Eli Lilly	3277

66

Data compiled by Dominic Golding   Main sources: OECD *Environmental Data Compendium* (1989); UNEP *Environmental Data Report* (1988/90); Lagadec (1982); Gittus (1988).

Accidents are usually characterized as unprecedented events. But as industrialization spreads and the products of industry become more toxic, 'accidents' are becoming a normal part of industrial culture.

UNION OF SOVIET SOCIALIST REPUBLICS

Novosibirsk 1979

1988   1988   1988

Chernobyl 1986

MONGOLIA

1983   1979   TURKEY

N KOREA   1980   1978
JAPAN   1974   1974
1979   1977   1970   1982
S KOREA

CYPRUS
LEBANON   SYRIA   IRAQ   IRAN   AFGHANISTAN   1988
ISRAEL   JOR   1979

1983   EGYPT

CHINA

1988   1988

TAIWAN   PACIFIC
OCEAN

PAKISTAN   1985   NEPAL   BHUTAN   1987   TAIWAN
1974   1977
1987

SAUDI ARABIA   BAHRAIN   1977
QATAR   U.A.E.
OMAN

Bhopal 1984   B DESH
INDIA   1980   MYANMAR   LAOS

1985
1988
1985

THAILAND   1980   CAM   VIETNAM
1981

PHILIPPINES

SUDAN   N S YEMEN
YEMEN
DJIBOUTI

ETHIOPIA
SOMALIA

1985   SRI LANKA   1979

MALDIVES

1985   BRUNEI
1986   MALAYSIA
SINGAPORE

INDIAN
OCEAN

UGANDA   KENYA
AIRE   B

TANZANIA

COMOROS

SEYCHELLES

1984   INDONESIA   PAPUA
NEW
GUINEA

1973   1970

AMBIA   MALAWI

WESTERN SAMOA

ZIMBABWE   S
MOZAMBIQUE   MADAGASCAR

FIJI

1973
SOUTH
AFRICA

AUSTRALIA

1982

NEW
ZEALAND

DEADLY INDUSTRY

MAJOR INDUSTRIAL ACCIDENTS
resulting in damage to human health, life and the
environment *1969-89*
date given where known

major   catastrophic
industrial   industrial
accident   accident

- manufacturing plant or
  storage facility accident

- transportation accident

- accident in natural gas/oil
  refining facility, pipeline or
  storage tank

- other accident in manufacture
  and transportation of
  hazardous materials

For oil spills and oil-rig blowouts, see Map 22

C A N A D A

UNITED STATES
OF AMERICA

PACIFIC
OCEAN

ATLANTIC OCEAN

□ BERMUDA

USA
MEXICO

USA
BAHAMAS

CUBA

BELIZE
GUATEMALA HONDURAS
EL SALVADOR
NICARAGUA

COSTA RICA
USA

PANAMA

USA
HAITI

DOMINICAN REPUBLIC
USA PUERTO RICO (US)

JAMAICA

GUADELOUPE (Fr)
DOMINICA
MARTINIQUE (Fr)
BARBADOS
TRINIDAD & TOBAGO

Italy
VENEZUELA

GUYANA
SURINAME
FRENCH GUIANA (Fr)

Netherlands

COLOMBIA

ECUADOR

B R A Z I L

PERU
USA USA

USA

BOLIVIA

PARAGUAY

USA

CHILE

USA
Uruguay

ARGENTINA

FALKLAND ISLANDS (Br)

□ ICELAND

NORWAY
USA
SWEDEN

USA USA
FINLAND

DENMARK
USA

USSR

IRELAND
USA Canada
Europe
UNITED
KINGDOM

EAST
GERMANY
W. Germany W. Germany
POLAND

W. Germany
NETH.
W. Europe

BEL
USA
LUX WEST
GERMANY
Netherlands

CZECH
AUSTRIA HUNGARY

W. Germany USA
FRANCE

W. Europe
Austria
ROMANIA

W. Germany
SWITZ.
ITALY
YUGOSLAVIA

W. Germany USA
BULGARIA

ALBANIA

GREECE

PORTUGAL

SPAIN

USA USA

GIBRALTAR (Br)

TUNISIA

W. Germany

MOROCCO

ALGERIA LIBYA

WESTERN SAHARA MAURITANIA
W. Germany

France
NIGER CHAD

SENEGAL
W. Germany
CAPE VERDE
GAMBIA
GUINEA-BISSAU
Europe
MALI
BURK
Europe

USSR
Italy USSR
NIGERIA

Egypt Italy
France

GUINEA
USA Norway
IVORY
COAST GHANA TOGO BENIN
CAMEROON
UK

SIERRA LEONE LIBERIA
USA UK

USA
Europe
EQUATORIAL GUINEA
SAO TOME & PRINCIPE GABON

ANGOLA

Switzerland

NAMIBIA
W. Germany

USA

TOXIC TRADE

MAJOR INTERNATIONAL TRADE IN
HAZARDOUS WASTE
1985-89

major exporters

major exporters, also
importing hazardous waste
from abroad

other importers, willing or
unwilling

other countries

DUMPING GROUNDS
Status of foreign hazardous waste
shipments
1985-89

shipments being received

dumping, legal or illegal,
known to have occurred

dumping rejected;
hazardous materials may
remain

shipments planned or under
consideration

attempt or proposal, status
unclear

For production of hazardous waste see
Map 25.

700

155 150

68

40
25 20 15
0.7

W Germany
Netherlands
USA
Switzerland
Canada
France
Ireland
Sweden
Australia

Average annual exports of
hazardous waste
mid-1980s thousand tonnes

OUT OF SIGHT

Data compiled by Marina Alberti   Main sources: Greenpeace (1989); OECD *Environmental Data Compendium* (1989).

Poor countries have become dumping grounds as industrialized countries try to ship their toxic wastes out of sight out of mind.

UNION OF SOVIET SOCIALIST REPUBLICS

MONGOLIA

Italy   W. Germany   W. Germany
TURKEY

CYPRUS   SYRIA   Italy
LEBANON   IRAQ
Italy   ISRAEL   JOR

CHINA

Europe   W. Germany   USA

N KOREA
S KOREA

USA   USA
JAPAN

PACIFIC
OCEAN

EGYPT

AFGHANISTAN

USA
PAKISTAN

IRAN

KUWAIT
BAHRAIN
QATAR
U.A.E.

W. Germany
SAUDI ARABIA

OMAN

INDIA

NEPAL   BHUTAN

B
DESH

MYANMAR   LAOS

TAIWAN

N
S YEMEN

SUDAN

DJIBOUTI

W. Germany

Italy
ETHIOPIA

Italy

SOMALIA

USA

MALDIVES

SRI LANKA

Singapore
THAILAND

CAM   VIETNAM

PHILIPPINES

USA

INDIAN OCEAN

BRUNEI

SINGAPORE

MALAYSIA

IRE

USA/Europe
KENYA

Switzerland   USA

SEYCHELLES

Europe
TANZANIA

COMOROS

INDONESIA

USA
PAPUA
NEW
GUINEA

MALAWI

BIA

COUNTRIES REFUSING HAZARDOUS WASTE IMPORTS

import ban in force, as of 1989

other countries

dumping proposal rejected 1985-89

USA
ZIMB

CHILE

WESTERN SAMOA

FIJI

UTH
RICA

MOZAMBIQUE

AUSTRALIA

USA

NO-GO AREAS

YUGOSLAVIA

TURKEY

BAHAMAS

MOROCCO

S KOREA

HAITI
DOMINICAN REP
ST. LUCIA
ANTIGUA

CAPE
VERDE

ALGERIA   LIBYA

TAIWAN

BELIZE

GUATEMALA   JAMAICA   BARBADOS
HONDURAS   TRINIDAD &
COSTA RICA   TOBAGO
PANAMA   GUYANA

SENEGAL
GAMBIA
GUINEA
BISSAU
GUINEA

NIGER

TOGO   NIGERIA

SUDAN

SRI LANKA

PHILIPPINES

SIERRA LEONE   BENIN

LIBERIA   CAMEROON
IVORY COAST
GHANA
GABON
CONGO

KENYA
BURUNDI
TANZANIA
COMOROS

SINGAPORE

INDONESIA

SOLOMON
ISLANDS

VENEZUELA

PERU

ZAMBIA

ZIMBABWE

VANUATU
WESTERN
SAMOA

NEW
ZEALAND

CHILE

AMERICAN
SAMOA

Copyright © Swanston Publishing Limited

GREENLAND
(Den)

ICELAND

NORWAY
SWEDEN

DENMARK

IRELAND
UNITED
KINGDOM
NETH
BEL
W GER
FRANCE
LIECHT

GER
POLA
CZECH
HUN
YUGOSLA

C A N A D A

UNITED STATES
OF AMERICA

ATLANTIC
OCEAN

PORTUGAL
SPAIN

TUNISIA

MOROCCO

ALGERIA

LIBYA

BERMUDA

WESTERN SAHARA

MEXICO

Bahamas

CUBA

HAITI
DOMINICAN REPUBLIC
PUERTO RICO (US)

MAURITANIA

M A L I

NIGER

CHA

BELIZE
GUATEMALA
EL SALVADOR
HONDURAS

JAMAICA

GUADELOUPE (Fr)
DOMINICA
MARTINIQUE (Fr)
BARBADOS

CAPE VERDE

SENEGAL
GAMBIA
GUINEA-BISSAU

BURKINA
GUINEA

BENIN

NIGERIA

CA

NICARAGUA
COSTA RICA
PANAMA

TRINIDAD & TOBAGO

SIERRA LEONE
LIBERIA

IVORY
COAST

GHANA
TOGO

CAMEROON

VENEZUELA
GUYANA
SURINAME
FRENCH GUIANA (Fr)

GABON
CONGO

COLOMBIA

ECUADOR

ANGO

PACIFIC
OCEAN

PERU

B R A Z I L

ATLANTIC
OCEAN

BOLIVIA

NAMIBIA

PARAGUAY

CHILE

URUGUAY

ARGENTINA

FALKLAND ISLANDS (Br)

HOLES IN THE SKY

CFC CONSUMPTION·PER PERSON
PER YEAR
mid-1980s averages
100 gm = 3.5 oz

- 500 gm
- 200 gm
- 100 gm

- data not available

MONTREAL PROTOCOL *1989*
to reduce ozone-damaging chemicals

- ● ratifying state
- ● non-ratifying signatory

For air quality see Map 17; for fossil fuel
pollution see Map 23.

DANGER ZONES

OZONE LOSS IN THE HEMISPHER
ANNUAL MEAN PERCENTAGES
1979-80 to 1987-88

- 9% loss
- 7.5% loss
- 6% loss
- 4.5% loss
- 3% loss
- 1.5% loss

- no annual readings

Data compiled by Nigel Dudley   Main sources: US Environmental Protection Agency (1986); NASA Ozone Trends Panel;
John Gille, US National Center for Atmospheric Research.

The chemicals that are now destroying the ozone layer do not occur naturally – they are entirely the creation of modern industry.

UNION OF SOVIET SOCIALIST REPUBLICS

MONGOLIA

TURKEY

CYPRUS
LEBANON
ISRAEL
SYRIA
JOR
IRAQ

KUWAIT
BAHRAIN
QATAR
UAE
SAUDI ARABIA
OMAN

EGYPT

N. YEMEN
S. YEMEN

DJIBOUTI

SUDAN

ETHIOPIA

SOMALIA

UGANDA
KENYA

TANZANIA

MALAWI

COMOROS

MOZAMBIQUE

MADAGASCAR

ZIMBABWE

BIA

RE

AFGHANISTAN

IRAN

PAKISTAN

NEPAL
BHUTAN

INDIA

B
DESH

SRI LANKA

MALDIVES

SEYCHELLES

INDIAN
OCEAN

CHINA

N. KOREA

S. KOREA

JAPAN

TAIWAN

MYANMAR

LAOS

THAILAND

CAM
VIETNAM

PHILIPPINES

BRUNEI

MALAYSIA

SINGAPORE

INDONESIA

PACIFIC
OCEAN

PAPUA
NEW
GUINEA

WESTERN SAMOA

FIJI

AUSTRALIA

NEW
ZEALAND

NORTHERN HEMISPHERE

SOUTHERN HEMISPHERE

CANADA

GREENLAND
(Den)

ICELAND

UNITED STATES
OF AMERICA

NORWAY
SWEDEN
DENMARK
UNITED
IRELAND   KINGDOM
NETH.
E.
BEL.   GER
CZECH
W. GER
AUS.
FRANCE
PORTUGAL   SPAIN
YUGOS.
ITALY

BERMUDA

ATLANTIC
OCEAN

TUNISIA

MOROCCO

ALGERIA

LIBY

MEXICO

BAHAMAS

CUBA
HAITI   DOMINICAN REPUBLIC
PUERTO RICO (US)
BELIZE
HONDURAS   JAMAICA
GUATEMALA
GUADELOUPE (Fr)
DOMINICA
MARTINIQUE (Fr)
NICARAGUA   BARBADOS
EL SALVADOR   COSTA RICA   TRINIDAD & TOBAGO
PANAMA

WESTERN
SAHARA

MAURITANIA

MALI

NIGER

CAPE VERDE

SENEGAL
GAMBIA
GUINEA-BISSAU   GUINEA
SIERRA LEONE   IVORY
COAST
LIBERIA

BURKINA

NIGERIA

GHANA
TOGO
BENIN

CH

VENEZUELA   GUYANA
SURINAME
FRENCH GUIANA (Fr)
COLOMBIA

ECUADOR

EQUATORIAL GUINEA
SAO TOME & PRINCIPE

CAMEROON

GABON
CONGO

PERU

BRAZIL

PACIFIC
OCEAN

BOLIVIA

PARAGUAY

CHILE

URUGUAY

ARGENTINA

ANG

NAMIE

WAR-WASTED LANDS

WHERE WARS ARE BEING FOUGHT,
1989
Number of years in progress

over 30 years

20 to 30 years

10 to 20 years

less than 10 years

ENVIRONMENTAL WAR DAMAGE
IN CENTRAL AMERICA *1980s*

main areas of conflict   air bases

scorched earth policy implemented
by government forces

MEXICO   BELIZE
HONDURAS
EL SALVADOR   NICARAGUA
COSTA
RICA

ECOCIDE

72

Data compiled by Dan Smith   Main sources: EPOCA (1989); SIPRI *Yearbook* (1987, 1988, 1989); Sivard (1989); Wallensteen (1988)

As the weapons of war become more powerful, so the environmental damage they cause escalates. Often the environment itself is a military target.

UNION OF SOVIET SOCIALIST REPUBLICS

MONGOLIA

CHINA

N.KOREA

S.KOREA

JAPAN

TURKEY

CYPRUS

SYRIA

LEBANON

JOR

IRAQ

IRAN

AFGHANISTAN

PAKISTAN

NEPAL

BHUTAN

KUWAIT

BAHRAIN

QATAR

U.A.E.

OMAN

EGYPT

ISRAEL

SAUDI ARABIA

INDIA

B.DESH

MYANMAR

LAOS

THAILAND

CAM

VIETNAM

PHILIPPINES

PACIFIC OCEAN

TAIWAN

SUDAN

N.YEMEN

S.YEMEN

DJIBOUTI

ETHIOPIA

SOMALIA

MALDIVES

SRI LANKA

BRUNEI

MALAYSIA

SINGAPORE

UGANDA

KENYA

AIRE

TANZANIA

SEYCHELLES

COMOROS

INDONESIA

PAPUA NEW GUINEA

MALAWI

MBIA

ZIMBABWE

MOZAMBIQUE

MADAGASCAR

INDIAN OCEAN

WESTERN SAMOA

FIJI

SOUTH AFRICA

AUSTRALIA

NEW ZEALAND

Copyright © Swanston Publishing Limited

CANADA

GREENLAND
(Den)

Amchitka
Is.
(USA)

(USA)

CANADA

(USA)

(USA)

Nevada
(USA)

Colorado (USA)

(USA)

(USA)

(USA)

(USSR)

HAWAII

New Mexico
(USA)

BERMUDA
(USSR)

(USA)

MEXICO

ICELAND

NORWAY

SWEDEN

DENMARK

IRELAND

UNITED
KINGDOM

NETH.

E
GER

POLA

W GER

CZECH

FRANCE

AUS.

HUN

YUGOSLA

(USSR)

PORTUGAL

SPAIN

ITALY

G

(USA)

MEXICO

CUBA

HAITI

JAMAICA

DOMINICAN REPUBLIC
PUERTO RICO (US)

GUADELOUPE (Fr)

DOMINICA

MARTINIQUE (Fr)

BARBADOS

TRINIDAD & TOBAGO

MOROCCO

TUNISIA

WESTERN SAHARA

ALGERIA

LIBYA

Reggan
(Fr.)

Inn Ekker
(Fr.)

BELIZE

GUATEMALA
EL SALVADOR

HONDURAS

NICARAGUA

COSTA RICA

PANAMA

VENEZUELA

GUYANA

SURINAME

FRENCH GUIANA (Fr)

COLOMBIA

ECUADOR

PERU

BRAZIL

BOLIVIA

PARAGUAY

CHILE

URUGUAY

ARGENTINA

CAPE VERDE

MAURITANIA

MALI

NIGER

CHA

SENEGAL

GAMBIA

GUINEA-BISSAU

GUINEA

SIERRA-LEONE

LIBERIA

IVORY
COAST

GHANA

TOGO

BENIN

NIGERIA

CA

CAMEROON

GABON

CONGO

ATLANTIC
OCEAN

PACIFIC
OCEAN

ANGOL

NAMIBIA

FALKLAND ISLANDS (Br)

NUCLEAR BLIGHT

POSSESSION OF NUCLEAR
WEAPONS AND BASES
1989

nuclear superpowers

other states possessing
nuclear weapons

states widely believed to
possess nuclear weapons

other states and territories
where nuclear weapons are
based

other

nuclear test sites
1989

former test sites

BLOTS ON THE SUPERPOWER
LANDSCAPE

Nuclear sites, production plants,
development centres or bases
late 1980s

USA

USSR

NUCLEAR BLIGHT

MILITARY NUCLEAR ACCIDENTS
Lost at sea *1950-89*

nuclear weapons

nuclear reactors

both weapons and reactors

74

Data compiled by Dan Smith   Main sources: Arkin and Fieldhouse (1985); Arkin and Handler (1989);
SIPRI Yearbooks

For non-military nuclear power see Map 19.

The nuclear activities of a few military states pose a real and present danger to the global environment.

GREENLAND
(Den)

ICELAND

NORWAY

SWEDEN

DENMARK

IRELAND   UNITED
           KINGDOM   NETH   E
                             GER   CZECH

BEL   W GER   AUS

FRANCE   YUGO

PORTUGAL   SPAIN   ITALY

C A N A D A

UNITED STATES
OF AMERICA

BERMUDA

ATLANTIC
OCEAN

TUNISIA

MOROCCO   ALGERIA   LIBY

WESTERN SAHARA

MEXICO

BAHAMAS

CUBA

HAITI   DOMINICAN REPUBLIC
         PUERTO RICO (US)

BELIZE
GUATEMALA   HONDURAS   JAMAICA   GUADELOUPE (Fr)
EL SALVADOR   DOMINICA
            NICARAGUA   MARTINIQUE (Fr)
                                       BARBADOS
COSTA RICA   TRINIDAD & TOBAGO
         PANAMA

MAURITANIA   M A L I   N I G E R   CH

CAPE VERDE   SENEGAL
              GAMBIA
              GUINEA-BISSAU
                    GUINEA
                           BURKINA   NIGERIA
SIERRA LEONE   IVORY   GHANA   CAMEROON
                COAST
         LIBERIA   TOGO BENIN
                                EQUATORIAL GUINEA
                                SAO TOME & PRINCIPE   GABON
                                                      CONGO   ANG

VENEZUELA   GUYANA
                   SURINAME
                   FRENCH GUIANA (Fr)
COLOMBIA

ECUADOR

PERU   B R A Z I L

PACIFIC
OCEAN

BOLIVIA

PARAGUAY

CHILE

URUGUAY

ARGENTINA

NAMIB

ATLANTIC
OCEAN

FALKLAND ISLANDS (Br)

AUTO CULTURE

RATIO OF PEOPLE TO CARS *1987*
One car for:

- fewer than 10 people
- 10-50 people
- 50-100 people
- 100-200 people
- more than 200 people
- data not available

Extremes: Bangladesh 2316 people per
car; USA 1.8 people per car; world
average: 12 people per car.

For air pollution see Maps 17 and 23.

Data compiled by Joni Seager   Main sources: *World Motor Vehicle Data* (1989).

The number of cars in the world has doubled in the past 20 years.

AUTO DEPENDANTS
Shares of the world's 400 million cars late 1980s

- Africa 1
- Oceania 2
- Canada 3
- USSR 3
- E. Europe 4
- rest of world 6
- USA 35
- L. America 7
- Japan 7
- W. Europe 32
- %

UNION OF SOVIET SOCIALIST REPUBLICS

MONGOLIA

TURKEY

CYPRUS
LEBANON
ISRAEL
SYRIA
IRAQ
JOR
KUWAIT
BAHRAIN
QATAR
U.A.E
SAUDI ARABIA
OMAN
N. YEMEN
S YEMEN
DJIBOUTI
GYPT
UDAN
ETHIOPIA
SOMALIA
UGANDA
KENYA
E
TANZANIA
COMOROS
MALAWI
MBABWE
MOZAMBIQUE
MADAGASCAR
IA
TH
A

AFGHANISTAN
IRAN
PAKISTAN
INDIA
NEPAL
BHUTAN
B
DESH
MYANMAR
LAOS
THAILAND
CAM
VIETNAM
SRI LANKA
MALDIVES
SEYCHELLES

CHINA

N KOREA
S KOREA
JAPAN

TAIWAN

PHILIPPINES

BRUNEI
MALAYSIA
SINGAPORE
INDONESIA
PAPUA NEW GUINEA

PACIFIC OCEAN

INDIAN OCEAN

WESTERN SAMOA
FIJI

AUSTRALIA

NEW ZEALAND

BIG WHEELS
The world's top 10 car manufacturers Shares of total world production 1987

- Volkswagen W Germany 7
- Peugeot Citroen France 7
- Nissan Japan 6
- Renault France 5
- Fiat Italy 5
- Toyota Japan 8
- Chrysler USA 4
- Honda Japan 4
- Ford USA 12
- General Motors USA 17
- all other manufacturers 25
- %

GREENLAND
(Den)

ICELAND

CANADA

NORWAY
SWEDEN
DENMARK
UNITED
KINGDOM
IRELAND
NETH
BEL
E GER
CZE
W GER
AUS
FRANCE
YUGO
ITALY

UNITED STATES
OF AMERICA

BERMUDA

ATLANTIC
OCEAN

PORTUGAL SPAIN

MOROCCO
TUNISIA

ALGERIA
LIB

MEXICO

BAHAMAS

WESTERN SAHARA

CUBA

HAITI
DOMINICAN REPUBLIC
PUERTO RICO (US)
BELIZE
JAMAICA
GUADELOUPE (Fr)
DOMINICA
MARTINIQUE (Fr)
BARBADOS
TRINIDAD & TOBAGO

MAURITANIA
MALI
NIGER

CAPE VERDE
SENEGAL
GAMBIA
GUINEA-BISSAU
GUINEA
BURKINA
NIGERIA
SIERRA LEONE
IVORY
COAST
GHANA
TOGO
BENIN
LIBERIA

GUATEMALA
EL SALVADOR
HONDURAS
NICARAGUA
COSTA RICA
PANAMA
VENEZUELA
GUYANA
SURINAME
FRENCH GUIANA (Fr)
COLOMBIA
ECUADOR

CAMEROON
EQUATORIAL GUINEA
SAO TOME & PRINCIPE
GABON
CONGO

PACIFIC
OCEAN

PERU

BRAZIL

TOURIST TRACKS

CHINA

Gamgadhi

ANG

Dhaulagiri
Everest
Parbat
NEPAL
Kathmandu

NAM

BOLIVIA

INDIA

TOURIST TRAPS

PARAGUAY

RATIO OF TOURISTS TO RESIDENTS
based on visitor arrival records *1987*

main trekking routes in Nepal

CHILE

more annual visitors than
residents

URUGUAY

as many visitors as
residents

ARGENTINA

Tourists to Nepal from abroad
1987

more residents than visitors

Europe 38%

Australia/New Zealand 5%

10 residents : 1 visitor

S Asia 24%

E Asia 16%

50 residents : 1 visitor

N America 13%

100 residents : 1 visitor

500 residents : 1 visitor

other
4%

data not available

FALKLAND ISLANDS (Br)

Extremes: St Maarten 34 visitor arrivals for
every 1 resident; Vietnam 1 visitor for every
8882 residents

Data compiled by Nigel Dudley and Mark Davis   Main sources: Commission of the European Communities *Quality of Bathing Water* (1987); World Tourism Organisation (1988).

The needs of tourists, especially rich tourists in poor countries, can deplete local resources and leave a global trail of litter and waste.

UNION OF SOVIET SOCIALIST REPUBLICS

MONGOLIA

CHINA

N KOREA

S KOREA

JAPAN

TURKEY

CYPRUS
LEBANON
ISRAEL
SYRIA
JOR
IRAQ

IRAN

AFGHANISTAN

KUWAIT

BAHRAIN

QATAR

U.A.E

OMAN

SAUDI ARABIA

N YEMEN
S YEMEN

DJIBOUTI

EGYPT

SUDAN

ETHIOPIA

SOMALIA

UGANDA

KENYA

TANZANIA

COMOROS

MALAWI

MOZAMBIQUE

MADAGASCAR

ZIMBABWE

SOUTH AFRICA

PAKISTAN

NEPAL

BHUTAN

INDIA

B DESH

MYANMAR

LAOS

THAILAND

CAM

VIETNAM

TAIWAN

PHILIPPINES

SRI LANKA

MALDIVES

SEYCHELLES

BRUNEI

MALAYSIA

SINGAPORE

INDONESIA

PAPUA NEW GUINEA

PACIFIC OCEAN

INDIAN OCEAN

AUSTRALIA

WESTERN SAMOA

FIJI

NEW ZEALAND

ON THE BEACH

BEACHES CONFORMING
TO NATIONAL STANDARDS
OF BACTERIA POLLUTION
1987 percentages

less than 75%

75-79%

80-85%

more than 85%

data not available

N Ireland

IRELAND

GREAT BRITAIN

DENMARK

NETH

BELGIUM

FRANCE
(excluding
Corsica)

PORTUGAL

SPAIN

Balearic Is.

Sardinia

Sicily

ITALY

YUGOSLAVIA

ALBANIA

GREECE

ICELAND

FINLAND

NORWAY
SWEDEN

USSR

IRELAND

UNITED
KINGDOM

DENMARK

NETH.

EAST
GERMANY

POLAND

BEL.

LUX.

WEST
GERMANY

CZECHOSLOVAKIA

ROMAN

SWITZ.

AUSTRIA

HUNGARY

C A N A D A

FRANCE

ITALY

YUGOSLAVIA

BULGA

PORTUGAL

SPAIN

ALBANIA

GREECE

UNITED STATES
OF AMERICA

GIBRALTAR (Br)

BERMUDA

ATLANTIC OCEAN

TUNISIA

MOROCCO

ALGERIA

LIBY

MEXICO

BAHAMAS

CUBA

HAITI

DOMINICAN REPUBLIC

JAMAICA

PUERTO RICO (US)

WESTERN SAHARA

MAURITANIA

NIGER

CHA

BELIZE
GUATEMALA
HONDURAS
EL SALVADOR
NICARAGUA

GUADELOUPE (Fr)

DOMINICA

MARTINIQUE (Fr)

BARBADOS

SENEGAL
GAMBIA
GUINEA-BISSAU

MALI

BURKINA

NIGERIA

COSTA RICA

PANAMA

VENEZUELA

TRINIDAD & TOBAGO

GUINEA

IVORY
COAST

GHANA

BENIN

CA

COLOMBIA

GUYANA

SURINAME

FRENCH GUIANA (Fr)

SIERRA LEONE
LIBERIA

TOGO

CAMEROON

ECUADOR

EQUATORIAL GUINEA

GABON

CONGO

PERU

B R A Z I L

ANGO

NAMIBI

BOLIVIA

PARAGUAY

PACIFIC
OCEAN

CHILE

URUGUAY

ARGENTINA

FALKLAND ISLANDS (Br)

THE WILD TRADE

MAJOR IMPORTERS OF WILDLIFE
annual trade mid-1980s

reptile skins
more than 75,000

live birds (mainly parrots)
more than 5000

live primates
more than 1000

Extremes: reptile skins USA (2.1m); live
birds USA (310,000); live primates USA
(16,000)

MAJOR EXPORTERS OF WILDLIFE
annual trade mid-1980s

reptile skins
more than 75,000

live birds (mainly parrots)
more than 5000

live primates
more than 1000

Extremes: reptile skins Argentina (1.3m);
live birds Argentina (179,500); live primates
Philippines (13,500)

For loss of mammal species see Map 3; for
hunting see Map 34.

Data compiled by Andy Crump   Main sources: World Resources Institute (1988); IUCN Monitoring Centre

The trade in wildlife and wildlife products is a $5 billion industry that threatens whole species and ecosystems.

☐ ICELAND

FINLAND

NORWAY

SWEDEN

capercaillie
(wood grouse)   sea eagle

DENMARK

USSR

IRELAND

UNITED
KINGDOM

European
otter

NETH

EAST
GERMANY

POLAND

BEL

LUX

WEST
GERMANY

CZECHOSLOVAKIA

griffon   red-billed
vulture   chough

FRANCE

SWITZ

AUSTRIA

HUNGARY

ROMAN

ITALY

YUGOSLAVIA

BULG

PORTUGAL

griffon vulture
SPAIN

ALBANIA

GREECE

European grey wolf

songbirds

GIBRALTAR (Br)

red-footed   cuckoo
falcon   songbird

MALT

polar bear

CANADA

Labrador
duck

grey wolf
grizzly bear
brown bear
cougar
jaguar
lynx

Pronghorn
antelope

black duck

UNITED STATES
OF AMERICA

☐ BERMUDA

Bermudan
cahow

BAHAMAS

ATLANTIC
OCEAN

MOROCCO

TUNISIA

skyla

jaguar   Kemp's
ridley turtle

MEXICO

CUBA

HAITI

DOMINICAN REPUBLIC
PUERTO RICO (US)

Edmi gazelle

LIBY

ALGERIA

WESTERN SAHARA

BELIZE

GUATEMALA

HONDURAS

JAMAICA

DOMINICA

MARTINIQUE (Fr)

GUADELOUPE (Fr)

MAURITANIA

MALI

Afri
eleph
black

scimitar-horned
oryx

Baird's tapir

EL SALVADOR

NICARAGUA

leather back
turtle

BARBADOS

TRINIDAD & TOBAGO

CAPE VERDE

SENEGAL

NIGER

CH

boa constrictor

COSTA RICA

PANAMA

VENEZUELA

GUYANA

SURINAME

FRENCH GUIANA (Fr)

GAMBIA

GUINEA-BISSAU

chimpanzee

GUINEA

BURKINA

IVORY
COAST

GHANA

BENIN

TOGO

NIGERIA

African elep
white

uakaris

COLOMBIA

SIERRA LEONE

LIBERIA

chimpanzee

CAMEROON

mandrill

EQUATORIAL GUINEA

SAO TOME & PRINCIPE

GABON

CONGO

ANGO

PACIFIC
OCEAN

ECUADOR

chimpanzee

PERU

emperor tamarin
uakaris

BRAZIL

mandrill
Abyssinian colobus
monkey

chinchilla
vicuna

uakaris

ATLANTIC
OCEAN

pygmy chimpanzee
mountain gorilla

chinchilla

BOLIVIA

PARAGUAY

African
elephant

NAMIBIA

CHILE

jackass
penguin

huemel

ARGENTINA

URUGUAY

bontebok
black
wildebeest

chinchilla
huemel

FALKLAND ISLANDS (Br)

HUNTING

WILDLIFE ENDANGERED BY
HUNTING *mid-1980s*

Endangered species

mammals

reptiles

birds

Species successfully recovering

mammals

birds

For loss of mammal species see Map 3; for
trade in wildlife see Map 33.

Data compiled by Andy Crump   Main sources: Burton & Pearson; Fitter (1986); Inskipp & Wells (1979); World Resources Institute (1987, 1988); OECD *Environmental Data
Compendium* (1989); IUCN Monitoring Centre (1988).

Hunting for sport or profit is one of the greatest threats to wildlife and wilderness ecosystems.

UNION OF SOVIET SOCIALIST REPUBLICS

Saiga antelope

MONGOLIA

snow leopard

N KOREA

S KOREA

amami rabbit

JAPAN

TURKEY

songbirds

bee-eater
CYPRUS
SYRIA
LEBANON
ISRAEL
JOR.
IRAQ

Latifi's viper

Persian fallow deer
Asiatic cheetah
IRAN

KUWAIT

BAHRAIN
QATAR
U.A.E.

AFGHANISTAN

PAKISTAN

NEPAL

BHUTAN

C H I N A

giant panda
Manchurian tiger
wild bactrian camel
brown bear

wild yak
snow leopard

Asiatic black bear

TAIWAN

PACIFIC OCEAN

turtle dove
quail

EGYPT

Houbara bustard
SAUDI ARABIA

OMAN

Houbara bustard

tiger

I N D I A

B DESH

Indian elephant
clouded leopard

LAOS

MYANMAR

THAILAND

VIETNAM

CAM

kouprey

kouprey

monkey eagle
PHILIPPINES

Arabian oryx
N YEMEN
S YEMEN

African elephant
white rhino
SUDAN

Abyssinian colobus monkey

ETHIOPIA

DJIBOUTI

SOMALIA

black rhino

Abyssinian colobus monkey

slender loris

Asiatic black bear

keelback snake

Kitti's hog-nosed bat

kouprey

BRUNEI

proboscis monkey

MALDIVES

loris

SRI LANKA

M A L A Y S I A

SINGAPORE

babirusa (wild hog)

fruit bat

PAPUA NEW GUINEA

UGANDA
KENYA

mountain gorilla
RWANDA

ZAIRE

TANZANIA

mountain gorilla

black rhino
Grevy's zebra

African elephant
white rhino

I N D I A N   O C E A N

black rhino
African elephant

INDONESIA

leatherback turtle

slow loris Javan pig swiftlet
Javan rhino
tiger

WESTERN SAMOA

FIJI

black rhino
MALAWI

ZIMBABWE

MOZAMBIQUE

aye-aye (lemur)
MADAGASCAR

koala bear

AUSTRALIA

SOUTH
AFRICA

black rhino
African hunting dog

WHALES AT RISK

ARCTIC OCEAN

bowhead

bowhead

ICELAND
NORWAY

UNION OF SOVIET
SOCIALIST REPUBLICS

sei

right

sperm   right   blue

S KOREA   JAPAN

sperm

blue
fin
humpback

gray

gray
sperm

fin
humpback

fin

Tasmanian
wolf

NEW
ZEALAND

INDIAN
OCEAN

PACIFIC OCEAN

ATLANTIC
OCEAN

blue

right   sei
humpback

fin

blue

MAJOR WHALE SPECIES
VULNERABLE TO EXTINCTION
mid-1980s

stable

highly endangered

endangered

whale-hunting countries
mid-1980s

□ ICELAND

NORWAY

FINLAND

SWEDEN

USSR

Asia 71%
Africa 27%
Latin America 2%

Asia 72%
Africa 21%
Latin America 7%

Asia 66%
Africa 18%
Latin America 16%

DENMARK

UNITED KINGDOM

NETH.

Latin America 3%
Asia 46%
Africa 51%

E GER

POLAND

Asia 54%
Africa 45%
Latin America <1%

BEL.

LUX.

CZECHOSLOVAKIA

Africa 82%
Asia 18%
Latin America <1%

WEST GERMANY

FRANCE

AUSTRIA

HUNGARY

ROMAN

Africa 99%
Asia <1%
Latin America <1%

SWITZ.

YUGOSLAVIA

BULG

CANADA

SPAIN

Africa 92%
Asia 5%
Latin America 3%

Africa 75%
Asia 24%
Latin America 1%

ITALY

ALBANIA

GREECE

PORTUGAL

GIBRALTAR (Br)

UNITED STATES
OF AMERICA

Asia 79%
Latin America 19%
Africa 2%

□ BERMUDA

MEXICO

TUNISIA

MOROCCO

ALGERIA

LIBY

BAHAMAS

CUBA

WESTERN SAHARA

HAITI

BELIZE

DOMINICAN REPUBLIC

PUERTO RICO (US)

JAMAICA

MAURITANIA

MALI

NIGER

CHA

GUATEMALA

HONDURAS

GUADELOUPE (Fr)

EL SALVADOR

DOMINICA

CAPE VERDE

SENEGAL

NICARAGUA

MARTINIQUE (Fr)

GAMBIA

BARBADOS

GUINEA-BISSAU

COSTA RICA

TRINIDAD & TOBAGO

GUINEA

BURKINA

PANAMA

VENEZUELA

GUYANA

SIERRA LEONE

IVORY
COAST

GHANA

BENIN

NIGERIA

COLOMBIA

SURINAME

FRENCH GUIANA (Fr)

LIBERIA

TOGO

CAMEROON

CA

ECUADOR

EQUATORIAL GUINEA

SAO TOME & PRINCIPE

GABON

CONGO

PERU

B R A Z I L

ATLANTIC
OCEAN

ANGO

BOLIVIA

NAMIBIA

PACIFIC
OCEAN

PARAGUAY

CHILE

URUGUAY

ARGENTINA

FALKLAND ISLANDS (Br)

84

Data compiled by Friends of the Earth/Jan McHarry   Main sources: Nectoux & Dudley (1987); Myers & Houghton (1989).

Every year tropical timber worth more than US$8 billion is shipped from poor countries to rich, destroying 12 million acres of tropical forest.

UNION OF SOVIET SOCIALIST REPUBLICS

MONGOLIA

N KOREA

JAPAN

S KOREA

Asia 97%
Africa 2%
Latin America 1%

CHINA

TURKEY

CYPRUS
LEBANON
ISRAEL JOR
SYRIA
IRAQ
IRAN
AFGHANISTAN

PACIFIC
OCEAN

KUWAIT
BAHRAIN
QATAR
U.A.E.

PAKISTAN

NEPAL
BHUTAN

TAIWAN

EGYPT

SAUDI ARABIA
OMAN

INDIA

B
DESH

MYANMAR

LAOS

N YEMEN
S YEMEN

THAILAND

CAM
VIETNAM

PHILIPPINES

SUDAN
DJIBOUTI

ETHIOPIA

SOMALIA

THE TIMBER TRADE

MAJOR EXPORTERS OF TROPICAL
TIMBER *1989*

UGANDA
KENYA

SEYCHELLES

major exporters

BRUNEI

MALAYSIA

major exporters *forests in
critical condition*

SINGAPORE

TANZANIA

major previous exporters
logged out early 1980s

MAJOR IMPORTERS OF TROPICAL
TIMBER *1989*

INDONESIA

PAPUA
NEW
GUINEA

COMOROS

MBIA
MALAWI

major importers

ZIMBABWE

MADAGASCAR

other countries

WESTERN SAMOA

FIJI

UTH
RICA

SIZE OF IMPORTS AND SOURCES
OF TIMBER *mid-1980s*
cubic metres roundwood equivalent

AUSTRALIA

over 2 million
percentages by region

1-2 million
percentages by region

NEW
ZEALAND

below 1 million
percentages by region

Extremes: world's largest importer: Japan;
world's largest exporter: Malaysia

For rainforest destruction see Map 5.

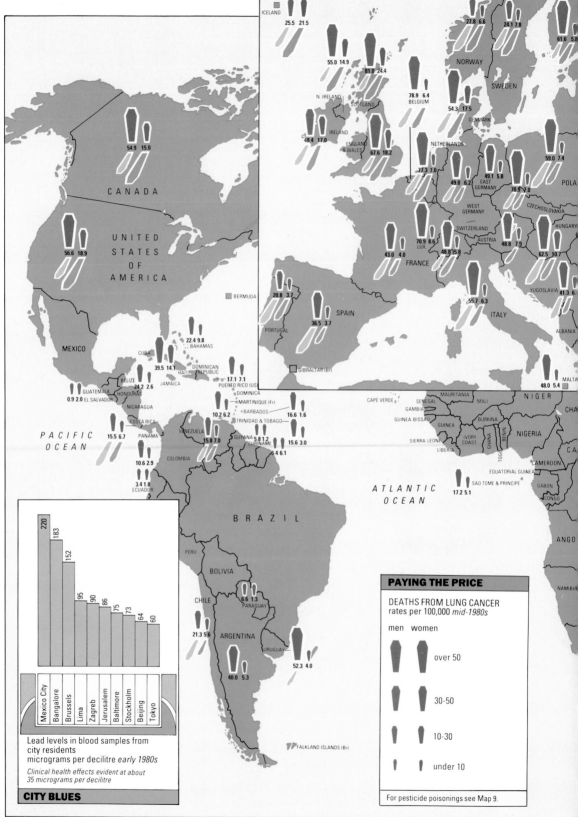

Copyright © Swanston Publishing Limited

CITY BLUES

Lead levels in blood samples from city residents
micrograms per decilitre *early 1980s*

Clinical health effects evident at about 35 micrograms per decilitre

Mexico City 220
Bangalore 183
Brussels 152
Lima 95
Zagreb 90
Jerusalem 86
Baltimore 75
Stockholm 73
Beijing 64
Tokyo 60

PAYING THE PRICE

DEATHS FROM LUNG CANCER
rates per 100,000 *mid-1980s*

men   women

over 50

30–50

10–30

under 10

For pesticide poisonings see Map 9.

Data compiled by Jean MacRae   Main sources: WHO, *World Health Statistics* (1988); Vater (1982).

The links between specific illnesses and environmental factors are difficult to prove. Nor can they be discounted. Smoking continues to be the most identifiable cause of lung cancer.

USSR

UNION OF SOVIET SOCIALIST REPUBLICS

56.3 10.2

MONGOLIA

CHINA

N.KOREA

S.KOREA 17.6 4.5

JAPAN 25.9 7.4

PACIFIC OCEAN

TURKEY

SYRIA
JOR
IRAQ
IRAN
AFGHANISTAN

PAKISTAN

NEPAL
BHUTAN

BULGARIA 3.7 6.4

4.1 5.8
ROMANIA

45.7 6.2

24.2 7.8
ISRAEL

KUWAIT 19.1 5.0
BAHRAIN
QATAR
U.A.E.

OMAN

INDIA

B.DESH

MYANMAR

TAIWAN

HONG KONG (Br) 55.5 23.1

38.5 10.7
BAHRAIN

SAUDI ARABIA

SUDAN

T.N
S.YEMEN
YEMEN
DJIBOUTI

ETHIOPIA

SOMALIA

UGANDA
KENYA

AIRE
B

TANZANIA

MALDIVES

2.0 0.7
SRI LANKA

LAOS

THAILAND

CAM

VIETNAM

PHILIPPINES

BRUNEI

MALAYSIA

SINGAPORE 59.5 18.9

INDONESIA

PAPUA NEW GUINEA

SEYCHELLES 76.0 18.3

COMOROS

INDIAN OCEAN

WESTERN SAMOA
FIJI

AMBIA
MALAWI
ZIMBABWE
MOZAMBIQUE

MADAGASCAR

14.8 4.3
MAURITIUS

AUSTRALIA

48.2 10.4

SOUTH AFRICA

PAYING THE PRICE

PERCENTAGE CHANGE IN LUNG CANCER DEATH RATES, where known

men   women

decrease

up to 50% increase

50–100%

100–200%

over 200%

NEW ZEALAND 49.7 13.7

ICELAND

FINLAND

from UK,
E. Germany

NORWAY

SWEDEN

Latvia,
Lithuania,
Estonia

nuclear and other
waste dumping
by UK

DENMARK

USSR

IRELAND

UNITED
KINGDOM

R.Weser

POLAND

Sellafield (UK)
radioactive waste
dumping

R. Schelde

NETH

R.Rhine

EAST
GERMANY

R.Elbe

NATO
manoeuvres

BEL

W.GER

CZECH

Czech nuclear power
plants

Creys-Malville

R. Maas

LUX

Kalkar

Cattenom

Wackersdorf
nuclear
reprocessing

SWITZ

AUSTRIA

HUNG

dams
R.Tisza

FRANCE

ITALY

R. Danube

ROMANIA

Alaska

YUGOSLAVIA

BULGARIA

C A N A D A

PORTUGAL

SPAIN

ALBANIA

GREECE

Alberta
missile testing

Saskatchewan
missile testing

NATO base
expansion

from US
power plants

Great Lakes

BERMUDA

Mono Lake

UNITED STATES
OF AMERICA

territorial disputes
and oil drilling

Medjerda R.

TUNISIA

Colorado R.

MOROCCO

Rio Grande

ALGERIA

LIBYA

from US
copper
plants

MEXICO

BAHAMAS

ATLANTIC
OCEAN

WESTERN SAHARA

CUBA

HAITI

DOMINICAN REPUBLIC
PUERTO RICO (US)

BELIZE

GUATEMALA
HONDURAS

JAMAICA

GUADELOUPE (Fr)

DOMINICA

MARTINIQUE (Fr)

trawler fishing by
European countries

MAURITANIA

MALI

NIGER

CHAD

EL SALVADOR

NICARAGUA

BARBADOS

CAPE VERDE

SENEGAL

COSTA RICA

TRINIDAD & TOBAGO

GAMBIA

GUINEA BISSAU

PANAMA

VENEZUELA

GUYANA

SURINAME

GUINEA

SIERRA LEONE

LIBERIA

IVORY
COAST

GHANA

TOGO

BENIN

NIGERIA

CA

COLOMBIA

FRENCH GUIANA (Fr)

CAMEROON

EQUATORIAL GUINEA

PACIFIC
OCEAN

ECUADOR

SAO TOME & PRINCIPE

GABON

CONGO

PERU

B R A Z I L

ATLANTIC
OCEAN

ANGOL

BOLIVIA

Lauca R.

NAMIBIA

A CLASH OF INTERESTS

CAUSES OF MAJOR
ENVIRONMENTAL PROTEST
1980s

PARAGUAY

CHILE

Parana R.

URUGUAY

water rights, water
diversions, water pollution

ARGENTINA

ocean pollution, fishing and
fishing rights

radioactive
waste dump

forest clearance, logging
and mining

acid rain pollution

nuclear power disputes
international only

military environmental
damage *international only*

FALKLAND ISLANDS (Br)

project postponed or
cancelled *as of 1989*

Data compiled by Michael Renner   Main sources: press reports.

Environmental issues are increasingly in
the foreground of relations between
citizens and their governments, and
between states.

Siberian Rivers

UNION OF SOVIET SOCIALIST REPUBLICS

MONGOLIA

Aral Sea

TURKEY

CYPRUS
LEBANON
ISRAEL

SYRIA

JOR

R.Tigris
R.Euphrates

IRAN

IRAQ KUWAIT

BAHRAIN

QATAR

U.A.E.

SAUDI ARABIA

OMAN

AFGHANISTAN

PAKISTAN

See inset

EGYPT

Nile

N
YEMEN

S.YEMEN

DJIBOUTI

SUDAN

ETHIOPIA

SOMALIA

UGANDA

KENYA

TANZANIA

COMOROS

MALAWI

MADAGASCAR

MOZAMBIQUE

ZIMBABWE

SEYCHELLES

INDIAN OCEAN

CHINA

N.KOREA

S.KOREA

JAPAN

driftnet fishing
by Japan, S. Korea,
Taiwan

PACIFIC
OCEAN

Three Gorges
dam

Nu Jiang R.

Brahmaputra R.

Daya Bay
nuclear power plant

TAIWAN

HONG KONG (Br)

R.Ganges

NEPAL

BHUTAN

INDIA

B.
DESH

Uttar
Pradesh

Narmada Valley
irrigation & hydro projects

Salween R.

MYANMAR

LAOS

VIETNAM

THAILAND

CAM.

Mekong R.

N. Luzon

Manila nuclear power plant

Karnataka

PHILIPPINES

SRI LANKA

MALDIVES

BRUNEI

MALAYSIA

SINGAPORE

driftnet fishing
by Japan, S. Korea,
Taiwan

INDONESIA

PAPUA
NEW
GUINEA

WESTERN SAMOA
nuclear
testing

FIJI

AUSTRALIA

Mururoa
Atoll
nuclear
testing

INSET:

TURKEY

CYPRUS

SYRIA

LEBANON

Yarmuk R.

IRAQ

West
Bank

R.Jordan

ISRAEL

JORDAN

SAUDI ARABIA

Franklin Tasmania
dam   pulp mill

NEW
ZEALAND

	1 Population 1989 millions	2 Population growth rate 1985-90 percentages	3 Urban population 1985 percentages of total population	4 Land area protected 1988 percentages of total land	5 Carbon dioxi emissions 1987 million tonn
Afghanistan	20.2	4.83	18.5	00.2	3.996
Albania	3.3	2.10	34.0	2.0	9.458
Algeria	24.7	3.21	42.6	0.2	3.666
American Samoa (US)			48.2		
Angola	9.7	2.67	24.5	1.2	4.399
Antigua & Barbuda			30.8		0.367
Argentina	32.4	1.46	84.6	1.7	109.247
Australia	16.5	1.25	85.5	4.7	234.257
Austria	7.5	0.01	56.1	5.1	52.057
Bahamas			57.5		1.100
Bahrain	0.5	3.72	81.7	0.0	16.130
Bangladesh	112.3	2.61	11.9	0.7	12.464
Barbados	0.3	0.60	42.2	05.8	0.733
Belgium	9.9	0.09	96.3	0.4	94.949
Belize			50.0		0.183
Benin	4.6	3.12	35.2	7.6	0.367
Bermuda					0.733
Bhutan	1.5	2.03	4.5	18.6	0.0
Bolivia	7.1	2.76	47.8	4.5	4.033
Botswana	1.3	3.70	19.2	17.0	1.466
Brazil	147.4	2.07	72.7	1.4	184.400
Brunei			57.7		2.933
Bulgaria	9.2	0.38	66.5	1.0	120.611
Burkina	7.7	2.65	7.9	2.5	0.367
Burundi	5.3	2.84	5.6	0.0	0.0
Cambodia	8.1	2.48	10.8	0.0	0.367
Cameroon	11.0	2.80	42.4	3.6	5.866
Canada	26.5	1.01	75.9	2.5	400.694
Cape Verde	0.4	2.36	5.3		
Central African Republic	2.8	2.42	42.4	6.3	0.367
Chad	5.5	2.44	27.0	0.1	0.367
Chile	12.8	1.52	83.6	17.1	25.662
China	1110.8	1.18	20.6	0.2	2092.553
Colombia	31.2	2.05	67.4	4.7	48.025
Comoros	0.5	3.08	25.2		
Congo	1.9	2.73	39.5	4.0	1.833
Costa Rica	2.9	2.44	49.8	8.9	2.200
Cuba	10.47	0.98	71.8	2.6	31.894
Cyprus	0.7	1.01	49.5	0.0	3.666
Czechoslovakia	15.8	0.32	65.3	14.4	234.257
Denmark	5.1	0.01	88.9	3.0	60.856

Sources: Col. 1: UN *World Population Prospects* (1988); **Col. 2:** UN *World Population Prospects* (1988); **Col. 3:** UN *Prospects of World Urbanization* (1988); **Col. 4:** World Resources Institute (1988); **Col. 5:** Oak Ridge National Laboratory; **Col. 6:** FAO *Fertilizer Yearbook* (1988); **Col. 7:** *World Motor Vehicle Data* (1989

INTERNATIONAL TABLE

6 Artificial fertilizer use 1987 kgs per hectare	7 Cars 1986-87 thousands	8 CITES signatories as of Jan.1990	9 Montreal Protocol signatories as of Dec.1989 □ non-ratifying	10 National Green Parties mid-1980s	11 Offices as of Jan.1990 Friends of the Earth Greenpeace W W F
9.7	33.0	●			
133.1					
38.0	589.0	●			
2.9	58.0				
	11.0				
4.5	4,060.0	●	□		G F
28.6	7,073.0	●	■		G F W
197.8	2,685.0	●	■	GP	G F W
50.0	68.0	●			
750.0	60.0				
77.0	45.0	●			F
93.9	35.0				
509.8	3,457.0	●	■	GP	G F W
81.8	0.5	●			
4.9	22.0	●			
	18.0				
1.0					
3.4	40.0	●			
<1.0	17.0	●			
53.2	10,827.0	●		GP	F
200.0	60.0				
180.4	1,100.0				
5.4	22.0		●		
2.0	7.5	●			
<1.0					
7.1	68.0	●	■		
48.1	11,500.0	●	■	GP	G F W
<1.0	43.0	●			
1.7	7.0	●			
52.3	591.0	●	□		
236.5	995.0	●			
94.8	579.0	●			
2.5	26.0	●	□		
180.6	114.0	●			G
197.0					
126.8	131.5	●			F
303.1	2,724.0				
233.5	1,588.0	●	■	GP	G F W

Col. 8: US State Department; **Col. 9:** US Environmental Protection Agency; **Col.10:** Sara Parkin, *Green Parties: An International Guide*, London: Heretic Books 1989; **Col. 11:** Friends of the Earth, London office; Greenpeace, Washington office; World Wildlife Fund, Washington office.

	1 Population 1989 millions	2 Population growth rate 1985-90 percentages	3 Urban population 1985 percentages of total population	4 Land area protected 1988 percentages of total land	5 Carbon dioxide emissions 1987 million tonnes
Djibouti	0.4	3.32	77.7	0.0	0.367
Dominica					0.0
Dominican Republic	6.8	2.21	55.7	11.8	6.599
Ecuador	10.5	2.79	52.3	38.4	13.931
Egypt	51.4	2.27	46.4	0.6	70.387
El Salvador	6.3	3.10	39.1	1.0	1.833
Equatorial Guinea	0.4	2.31	59.7	0.0	0.0
Ethiopia	48.7	2.79	11.6	1.6	2.566
Fiji	0.7	1.59	41.2	0.3	0.733
Finland	5.0	0.30	84.0	2.6	52.424
France	55.3	0.31	73.4	8.7	335.439
French Guiana			72.6		0.367
Gabon	1.2	2.01	40.9	6.8	5.132
Gambia	0.7	2.13	20.1	0.0	0.0
East Germany	16.9	0.15	77.0	0.7	324.074
West Germany	60.4	0.18	85.5	11.3	652.915
Ghana	15.5	3.36	31.5	5.1	2.933
Greece	10.0	0.41	60.1	1.1	52.424
Greenland (Den)			76.8		0.367
Guadeloupe (Fr)			45.7		0.733
Guatemala	8.9	2.88	40.0	0.9	2.566
Guinea	6.7	2.48	22.2	0.1	1.100
Guinea-Bissau	1.0	2.08	27.1	0.0	0.0
Guyana	1.0	1.74	32.2	0.1	1.100
Haiti	7.3	2.62	27.2	0.4	0.733
Honduras	5.0	3.10	40.0	3.2	1.466
Hong Kong (Br)			92.4		26.395
Hungary	10.7	0.07	56.2	4.8	74.420
Iceland	0.3	0.95	89.4	7.9	1.833
India	813.4	1.72	25.5	4.3	542.201
Indonesia	178.5	1.74	25.3	7.5	120.978
Iran	49.9	2.77	51.9	1.9	139.308
Iraq	18.2	3.31	70.6	0.0	42.892
Ireland	3.8	1.26	57.0	0.3	27.495
Israel	4.5	1.65	90.3	1.7	28.595
Italy	57.5	0.09	67.4	2.5	355.969
Ivory Coast	11.3	3.45	42.0	6.2	4.766
Jamaica	2.5	1.52	53.8	0.0	5.866
Japan	123.3	0.51	76.5	6.1	885.339
Jordan	4.1	3.99	64.4	0.4	8.798
Kenya	24.4	4.20	19.7	5.4	4.399

Sources: Col. 1: UN *World Population Prospects* (1988); **Col. 2**: UN *World Population Prospects* (1988); **Col. 3**: UN *Prospects of World Urbanization* (1988); **Col. 4**: World Resources Institute (1988); **Col. 5**: Oak Ridge National Laboratory; **Col. 6**: FAO *Fertilizer Yearbook* (1988); **Col. 7**: *World Motor Vehicle Data* (1989)

INTERNATIONAL TABLE

6 Artificial fertilizer use 1987 kgs per hectare	7 Cars 1986-87 thousands	8 CITES signatories as of Jan.1990	9 Montreal Protocol signatories as of Dec.1989 □ non-ratifying	10 National Green Parties mid-1980s	11 Offices as of Jan.1990 Friends of the Earth Greenpeace W W F
	15.0				
176.5	3.0				
55.6	103.0	●			
32.1	257.0	●			F
350.5	417.0	●	■		
126.2	73.0	●			
	4.5				
3.9	41.0	●			
89.6	31.0		■		
216.3	1,699.0	●	■	GP	G W
299.0	21,950.0	●	■	GP	G F W
166.7					
3.5	16.0	●			
15.3	5.0	●	■		
337.3	3,462.0	●	■	GP	G F
420.7	28,304.0	●	■	GP	G F W
3.8	60.0	●	■		F
170.6	1,433.0		■	GP	
142.9					
67.9	175.0	●	■		
<1.0	12.0	●			
<1.0	3.0				
26.9	33.0	●			
2.5	35.0				
23.1	41.0	●			
	184.0				F W
259.5	1,660.0	●	■		
2917.1	113.0		■	GP	
53.6	1,471.0	●			W
106.8	1,060.0	●	□		F
65.8	1,600.0	●			
39.7	376.0				
681.5	737.0		■	GP	G F
223.7	649.0	●	□		
190.1	22,800.0	●	■	GP	G F W
6.0	164.0				
91.4	93.0				
432.7	29,478.0	●	■	GP	G F W
34.8	136.0	●	■		
40.6	126.0	●	■		

Col. 8: US State Department; **Col. 9:** US Environmental Protection Agency; **Col. 10:** Sara Parkin, *Green Parties: An International Guide*, London: Heretic Books, 1989; **Col. 11:** Friends of the Earth, London office; Greenpeace, Washington office; World Wildlife Fund, Washington office.

	1 Population 1989 millions	2 Population growth rate 1985-90 percentages	3 Urban population 1985 percentages of total population	4 Land area protected 1988 percentages of total land	5 Carbon dioxid emissions 1987 million tonne
Kiribati			33.5		
North Korea	22.4	2.36	63.8	0.0	143.707
South Korea	44.1	1.89	65.3	5.7	162.770
Kuwait	2.1	4.15	93.5	0.0	32.994
Laos	4.5	2.43	15.9	0.0	0.0
Lebanon	2.9	2.13	80.1	0.0	8.065
Lesotho	1.7	2.61	16.7	0.2	
Liberia	2.5	3.25	39.5	1.4	0.733
Libya	4.2	3.67	64.5	0.1	24.929
Luxembourg	0.4	0.10	81.0	44.2	8.432
Madagascar	11.2	2.90	21.8	1.8	0.733
Malawi	7.9	3.32	12.0	11.3	0.367
Malaysia	17.0	2.12	38.2	4.9	40.326
Maldives			20.2		
Mali	9.1	2.94	18.0	0.7	0.367
Malta	0.4	0.66	85.3	0.0	0.0
Mauritania	2.1	3.08	34.6	1.4	3.299
Mauritius	1.1	1.65	42.4	2.0	1.100
Martinique (Fr)			71.1		0.733
Mexico	87.0	2.39	69.6	0.5	287.414
Mongolia	2.1	2.74	50.8	0.2	9.165
Morocco	24.1	2.30	44.8	0.7	18.330
Mozambique	15.5	2.69	19.4	0.0	0.733
Myanmar (Burma)	40.1	1.89	23.9	0.0	5.499
Namibia			51.3		
Nepal	18.1	2.28	7.7	7.1	131.976
Netherlands	14.7	0.34	88.4	4.4	0.733
New Zealand	3.4	0.86	83.7	11.4	20.896
Nicaragua	3.7	3.36	56.6	0.4	2.200
Niger	6.9	3.01	16.2	0.3	0.733
Nigeria	109.4	3.49	23.0	1.1	55.357
Norway	4.2	0.17	72.8	4.1	43.992
Oman	1.4	3.18	8.8	0.3	21.629
Pakistan	109.7	2.23	29.8	9.4	47.771
Panama	2.4	2.07	52.4	10.9	2.566
Papua New Guinea	3.9	2.38	14.3	0.4	2.200
Paraguay	4.1	2.78	44.4	2.8	1.833
Peru	21.8	2.51	67.4	4.2	22.363
Philippines	59.7	2.25	39.6	1.7	34.460
Poland	38.3	0.70	61.0	5.5	460.083
Portugal	10.5	0.64	31.2	4.2	27.862

Sources: Col. 1: UN *World Population Prospects* (1988); **Col. 2**: UN *World Population Prospects* (1988); **Col. 3**: UN *Prospects of World Urbanization* (1988); **Col. 4**: World Resources Institute (1988); **Col. 5**: Oak Ridge National Laboratory; **Col. 6**: FAO *Fertilizer Yearbook* (1988); **Col. 7**: *World Motor Vehicle Data* (1989)

INTERNATIONAL TABLE

6 Artificial fertilizer use 1987 kgs per hectare	7 Cars 1986-87 thousands	8 CITES signatories as of Jan.1990	9 Montreal Protocol signatories as of Dec.1989 □ non-ratifying	10 National Green Parties mid-1980s	11 Offices as of Jan.1990 Friends of the Earth Greenpeace W W F
311.7					
422.4	844.0				
82.0	435.0				
<1.0	10.0				
67.1					
12.5	6.0				
7.3		●			
28.8	404.0				
	162.0	●	■	GP	G
5.9	49.0	●			
20.4	16.0	●			
159.6	1,269.0	●	■		F W
			■		
13.9	21.0				
45.9		●	■		
5.0	15.0				
306.9	35.0	●			
1150.0					
75.3	5,403.0		■		
18.4					
35.7	565.0	●	□		
2.1	87.0	●			
15.4	35.0				
22.9		●			
687.9	5,118.0	●	■	GP	G F W
708.6	1,424.0	●	■	GP	G F W
43.3	32.0	●			F
<1.0	23.5	●			
9.9	774.0	●	■		
270.4	1,623.0	●	■	GP	G W
91.7	109.0				
82.9	273.0	●			F W
65.7	104.0	●	■		
38.1	17.0	●			F
4.4	88.5	●			
62.2	390.5	●			
65.0	359.0	●	□		
222.4	4,000.0				F
102.6	1,290.0	●	■		F

Col. 8: US State Department; Col. 9: US Environmental Protection Agency; Col. 10: Sara Parkin, *Green Parties: An International Guide*, London: Heretic Books 1989; Col. 11: Friends of the Earth, London office; Greenpeace, Washington office; World Wildlife Fund, Washington office.

	1 Population 1989 millions	2 Population growth rate 1985-90 percentages	3 Urban population 1985 percentages of total population	4 Land area protected 1988 percentages of total land	5 Carbon dioxide emissions 1987 million tonnes
Puerto Rico (US)			70.7		14.297
Qatar	0.4	5.44	88.0	0.0	11.365
Romania	23.7	0.68	49.0	0.6	205.663
Rwanda	6.9	3.36	6.2	10.5	0.367
Saudi Arabia	13.5	3.84	72.4	0.2	164.603
Senegal	7.2	2.71	36.4	11.3	1.833
Sierra Leone	3.9	1.93	28.3	1.4	0.733
Singapore	2.7	1.09	100.0	4.3	28.228
Solomon Islands	0.3	3.96	9.7	0.0	
Somalia	5.1	2.11	34.1	0.5	1.100
South Africa	35.8	2.53	55.9	4.7	278.249
Spain	39.5	0.62	75.8	3.4	161.304
Sri Lanka	17.2	1.48	21.1	10.6	3.666
Sudan	24.2	2.89	20.6	0.9	3.299
Suriname	0.4	1.46	45.7	4.6	1.100
Swaziland	0.7	3.14	26.3	2.3	0.367
Sweden	8.3	0.11	83.4	4.2	56.800
Switzerland	6.4	0.04	58.2	3.0	38.126
Syria	12.2	3.69	49.5	0.0	2.200
Taiwan					
Tanzania	26.1	3.65	22.3	12.0	25.662
Thailand	54.8	1.61	19.8	7.8	52.790
Togo	3.3	3.06	22.1	8.5	0.0
Trinidad & Tobago	1.3	1.59	63.9	3.1	17.597
Tunisia	7.7	2.17	56.8	0.4	9.898
Turkey	53.6	2.06	45.9	0.3	122.444
Uganda	17.8	3.49	9.5	6.7	0.733
United Arab Emirates	1.5	3.46	77.8	0.0	50.224
United Kingdom	56.2	0.02	91.5	6.4	569.696
USA	246.3	0.86	73.9	7.4	4457.123
USSR	289.3	0.93	65.6	0.0	3745.552
Uruguay	3.1	0.76	84.6	0.2	2.933
Venezuela	19.2	2.61	86.6	8.4	95.316
Vietnam	64.8	2.05	20.3	0.6	18.330
Western Sahara			52.9		0.367
South Yemen	2.4	3.01	39.9	1.3	2.933
North Yemen	7.7	2.92	20.0	0.8	5.499
Yugoslavia	23.8	0.63	46.3	1.3	120.611
Zaire	33.8	3.04	36.6	3.9	3.299
Zambia	7.6	3.43	49.5	8.6	2.200
Zimbabwe	10.1	3.61	24.6	7.1	15.397

Sources: Col. 1: UN *World Population Prospects* (1988); **Col. 2:** UN *World Population Prospects* (1988); **Col. 3:** UN *Prospects of World Urbanization* (1988); **Col. 4:** World Resources Institute (1988); **Col. 5:** Oak Ridge National Laboratory; **Col. 6:** FAO *Fertilizer Yearbook* (1988); **Col. 7:** *World Motor Vehicle Data* (1989)

INTERNATIONAL TABLE

6 Artificial fertilizer use 1987 kgs per hectare	7 Cars 1986-87 thousands	8 CITES signatories as of Jan.1990	9 Montreal Protocol signatories as of Dec.1989 □ non-ratifying	10 National Green Parties mid-1980s	11 Offices as of Jan.1990 Friends of the Earth Greenpeace WWF
	1,280.0				
172.5	78.0				
130.1	250.0				
2.0	7.0	●			
367.8	2,245.0				
4.0	78.0	●	□		
<1.0	23.0				F
1833.3	236.0	●	■		
4.0	17.0	●			
53.8	3,079.0	●			W
98.9	10,219.0	●	■		G F W
113.1	148.0	●			
2.5	34.0	●			
161.6	35.0	●			
39.6	21.0				
135.7	3,367.0	●	■	GP	G F W
430.6	2,733.0	●	■	GP	G F W
40.5	95.0		■		
	1,255.0				
8.9	42.0	●			F
29.3	572.0	●	■		
7.5	3.5	●	□		
52.5	264.0	●	■		
22.2	171.0	●	■		
61.8	193.0				
<1.0	32.0		■		
163.2	250.0	●			
355.5	20,097.0	●	■	GP	G F W
93.3	137,324.0	●	■		G F W
117.8	11,800.0	●	■		G F
42.7	164.0	●			F
158.0	1,601.0	●	■		
62.9					
12.1	12.0				
5.8	121.0				
132.8	3,040.0			GP	
<1.0	94.0	●			
18.4	98.0	●			
50.4	254.0	●			

Col. 8: US State Department; **Col. 9:** US Environmental Protection Agency; **Col. 10:** Sara Parkin, *Green Parties: An International Guide*, London: Heretic Books 1989; **Col. 11:** Friends of the Earth, London office; Greenpeace, Washington office; World Wildlife Fund, Washington office.

COMMENTARY

1 A GLOBAL GREENHOUSE

Certain gases, including carbon dioxide, methane, nitrogen oxides and chlorofluorocarbons (CFCs), are accumulating in the upper atmosphere at a faster rate than ever before. Proponents of the theory of global warming warn that this mixture is creating a layer that traps the earth's radiated heat, which will cause global temperatures to rise significantly. It is argued that this could lead to a rise in sea levels, higher tides and extraordinary storm surges; and the impact of these changes would mean salination of drinking water supplies, disruption of food crop and plant habitats, the expansion of deserts and the inundation of entire islands. Low-lying countries such as Bangladesh, the Netherlands, the Maldives and many small Pacific island states are especially vulnerable. Most of the world's major cities, including many capitals, are coastal and even a slight rise in sea-level would bring some threat of flooding. At a more extreme level, large-scale changes to weather and agricultural patterns would wreak havoc with local livelihoods and national economies.

Environmentalists are mapping out strategies to stave off global warming. These focus on the need for cutbacks in the use of fossil fuels (see Maps 23 and 31) and CFCs (see Map 28), as well as the need to call a halt to further global deforestation (see Maps 5 and 35). Such an agenda has sweeping implications. It would require dramatic changes in the priorities of industrial economies and industrial lifestyles; more difficult still is its potential impact on the plans of poor countries for economic expansion. The enormity of the demands is paralysing political and economic agreements and creating an uproar in scientific circles. But business and governments have short-term vested interests which make it convenient to dispute the theory of global warming.

Sources for map and commentary:
Boyle, Stewart & John Ardill, *The Greenhouse Effect*, London: New English Library, 1989; Hansen, J. et al, 'Global Climate Changes as Forecast by the Goddard Institute for Space Studies'. *Journal of Geophysical Research*, vol. 93, 1988; *Climatic Change, Rising Sea Level and the British Coast*, Institute of Terrestrial Ecology, NERC, 1989; Stevens, William, 'Adapting to Global Greenhouse', *International Herald Tribune*, November 16, 1989; World Resources Institute/International Institute for Environment and Development, *World Resources 1988-89*, New York: Basic Books, 1988.

2 A POPULAR PLANET

In 1985, Africa and Europe were approximately the same size in population; by 2025, Africa's population will be three times larger than that of Europe. Nigeria alone will grow from being half the population size of the USA to being slightly larger. In the mid-1980s, the Middle East dominated the ranks of states with the highest population growth rates: Oman, Libya, UAE, Qatar, Saudi Arabia, Kuwait, Bahrain, and Iran were all in the top ten. Dramatic increases such as these, together with the shifting relationships within the global population balance, form the backdrop to many of the environmental themes in this atlas.

But the relationship between population and the environment is complex. Some would argue, including some environmentalists, that there is a direct correlation between the world's growing population and the world's growing environmental problems. The evidence does not bear this out. While population growth is now a Third World phenomenon, the large-scale global environmental crises we face are largely the product of the voracious resource appetites of industrial economies and lifestyles. In terms of how much we burden the atmosphere, one economist estimates that the 'cost' of one US citizen is 16 times that of a Third World person; of a West European, five times. The average person in the developed world consumes 10 times as much energy, 10 times as much steel, 15 times as much paper, and one-and-a-half times as much food as does the average person living in the Third World. If we check off the world's most pressing environmental problems – fossil fuel pollution (and the related threat of global warming), the use and production of ozone depleting chemicals, the resource use and pollution generated by oil dependency, acid rain emissions, production of household waste, municipal waste, toxic industrial waste, the luxury trade in exotic animal and bird species, and the stripping of the world's forests – it becomes clear that the biggest **99** contributing cause of these problems is not the 'excessive' number of people in the poor countries of the world, but the excessive pressures exerted by the richer countries.

This is not to suggest that growing numbers of people do not burden natural ecosystems; they do. Destruction of wildlife habitats, forest cutback for subsistence agriculture and deterioration in the quality of urban water, to name but a few pressing environmental problems, stem in some measure from the sheer pressure of human need. Ultimately, though, most of these are problems of poverty and misdirected public priorities rather than problems of numbers. Military priorities are often the biggest stumbling block. For the cost of a single British Aerospace Hawk aircraft, for example, 1.5 million people in the Third World could have clean water for life; the annual cost of the proposed anti-desertification programme for Ethiopia is the equivalent of two months of Ethiopian military spending.

In turn, environmental problems themselves, in a world of social inequities, encourage high rates of population growth - in countries where infants die regularly from gastro-intestinal disease brought on by lack of clean water, for example, women have to bear higher numbers of children simply to meet perceived population replacement levels.

Population growth may well be a 'problem', but not in the ways that most of us are encouraged to believe. And the solution to environmental problems is not simply, or even primarily, through population controls; indeed, the reverse may well be true.

Sources for map and commentary:
Dankelman, Irene & Joan Davidson, *Women and Environment in the Third World*, London: IUCN/Earthscan, 1988; Greanville, Patrice, 'Who's Got the Answer to the Overpopulation Riddle?' *Animals' Agenda*, November 1988; United Nations, Department of International Economic and Social Affairs, *World Population Prospects, 1988*, 1989; World Commission on Environment and Development, *Our Common Future*, Oxford: Oxford University Press, 1987.

3 A SHRINKING WORLD

Overexploitation, loss of habitat (particularly through deforestation), hunting and the luxury trade in animals are the major causes of the spiralling scale of animal extinctions. By the year 2000, between 40,000 to 50,000 species will be lost annually.

Information about the world's animal communities is very uneven. As with plant species, more is generally known for richer, industrialized countries. Many others, including a number rich in both animal and plant species such as Brazil or Zaire, have little in the way of scientific monitoring services. The data is uneven in other important respects. More money is available to fund studies of large mammals and primates (perhaps because of perceived kinship and 'usefulness' to humans). Little attention is given to less attractive animals and birds and even less to fish or insects. There are only broad estimates for losses of fish and although many insect species are disappearing there is not even a 'best estimate' for the number becoming extinct.

Birds are especially vulnerable to extinction because they are migratory and range over a wide territory. There needs to be coordinated international action for the protection of birds but this will be difficult to achieve. For example, the annual hunting massacre of millions of songbirds along their migration paths in the Mediterranean has gained considerable notoriety and drawn protests from the EEC. It has not yet been halted. A third of Europe's birds are threatened with extinction, of which hunting is major cause, followed by habitat destruction. Hunters kill an estimated 900 million migrating birds each year. They justify this slaughter as a male ritual with links to cultural traditions that go back thousands of years.

Environmentalist Norman Myers comments wryly on the path down which we seem to be rushing: 'Unwittingly for the most part, but right around the world, we are eliminating the panoply of life. We elbow species off the planet, we deny room to entire communities of nature, we domesticate the Earth. With growing energy and ingenuity, we surpass ourselves time and again to exert dominion over fowl and fish ... Eventually we may achieve our aim, by eliminating every other competitor for living space on the crowded Earth. When the last creature is accounted for, we shall have made ourselves masters of all creation. We shall look around and we shall see nothing but each other. Alone at last.'

Sources for map and commentary:
Cocker, Mark, 'The Fall of Europe's Birds', *The Guardian* (London) July 25, 1989; IUCN Conservation Monitoring Centre, *Red List of Threatened Animals*, Cambridge: IUCN, 1988; Myers, Norman, ed., Gaia: *An Atlas of Planet Management*, London: Pan; New York: Doubleday, 1984; Organization for Economic Cooperation and Development (OECD), *OECD Environmental Data Compendium, 1989*, Paris: OECD, 1989; World Resources Institute/International Institute for Environment and Development, *World Resources 1988-89*, New York: Basic Books, 1988.

4 CUTTING OUR ROOTS

All life on the planet depends, directly or indirectly, on plants. And yet plants and plant species are being destroyed at an alarming rate. If present rates of habitat destruction continue, then some 40,000 - 60,000 vascular plants will face extinction within the next fifty years. In this map, we have included as much information as possible on small islands because they have distinctive biomes, tend to be rich in plant species and are suffering high rates of loss.

Beyond broad assessments, detailed information about plant extinctions is patchy. The Threatened Plants Unit of the International Union for Conservation of Nature (IUCN) in the UK collects the only available international database on plants, and publishes a floristic inventory in their Red Data Books. To date, Red Books have been compiled for 70 countries and islands. Most countries of the North, with predominantly temperate vegetation, are well covered by IUCN data, but there are few Red Books for countries of the South, where the vegetation is mostly tropical - and where most of the world's plants grow. There is almost no plant inventory or assessment for key areas such as Brazil, much of Central America and most of Africa. In the case of plant ecology, what we do not know is more problematic than what we do know. In general, it must be assumed that low rates of extinction reflect a lack of data more than they reflect the reality of plant losses.

The destruction of plants will threaten the world's food supplies and undermine medical advances. Wild plants are being lost which are needed to protect and maintain the world's major food crops. Eighty percent of our food comes from these crops and they are already suffering a dramatic decline in genetic diversity (see Map 10). Four-fifths of the world's population depends on natural plant sources for medicines. Even high-technology Western medicine uses a very high proportion of life-saving drugs that are initially derived from plant sources and then synthesized for large-scale production.

Sources for map and commentary:
Nature Conservancy Council, 'British Rare Plants: Threats and International Responsibilities', Data Support for Education, Sheet 60, 1989, Peterborough (UK) 1989; Davis, S.D., et al, *Plants in Danger: What do we Know?* Cambridge: IUCN, 1986; Fagan, Mary, 'Food Supply at Risk from Extinction of Plant Species', *The Independent* (London) December 16, 1989; World Resources Institute/International Institute for Environment and Development, *World Resources 1988-89*, New York: Basic Books, 1988.

5 RAINFOREST

Tropical forest originally covered about 16 million sq. kms. throughout the world; today, probably less than half remains. Although tropical forest (including rainforest) accounts for only a third of the world's total forest, it contains four-fifths of the world's vegetation: a single hectare of primary forest may support plant material weighing anywhere from 300 to 500 tonnes. More than that, it provides the habitat for about 50 percent of all animal and bird species. As tropical forest is destroyed, so other plant and animal life will disappear too. The recent recognition that tropical forests influence the global climate, and in particular may slow down the effects of global warming, has raised the stakes around tropical forest protection. However, to put an end to tropical deforestation will require strict regulation of multinational agricultural and logging industries. Although sustained international cooperation is essential, as well as a radical shift in the primary-resource economies of many countries, as of early 1990 there is still no international coordinating body.

The geography of rainforest has never been precise and reliable information on rates of deforestation does not exist. There are both practical and technical difficulties. One of these is the varying definitions of tropical forest, such as lowland, montane, dry, rain, swamp and so on. Further, when measuring deforestation, it is difficult to determine the difference between 'degraded' forest land and totally destroyed forest, especially since the one usually leads to the other. The term 'deforestation' itself means different things to different people. To commercial interests, deforestation means the loss of commercial timber stock. To environmentalists, deforestation is the destruction of an entire forest ecosystem, even though stands of trees may remain.

Whatever the definition, at the current rate of deforestation virtually all remaining tropical forests will disappear within 40 years. The tropical forests of the Ivory Coast, Nigeria, India, and Thailand are already severely depleted. By 2010, there will be very little forest left in Asia, and East and West Africa and almost none in Central America. Even in South America, the only large stands will remain in western Brazil and the highlands of Guyana.

Rainforest destruction has highlighted an important issue of social justice: the land rights of indigenous peoples. Large numbers of tribal people are each year losing their lands in the name of development and progress, and in the heart of Borneo, Brazil, the Philippines, and Malaysia, tribal peoples have been fighting a virtual life and death struggle to protect their rainforest homelands. Indigenous peoples and environmentalists are forming alliances to protect them.

There are many widely-accepted causes of rainforest loss: logging by commercial timber companies (see Map 35); migration of poor agricultural families into forests, often as part of government-promoted relocation schemes; conversion of forest land into commercial cash cropland, usually to grow beef or soya, and often to raise capital to pay off foreign debts; and firewood collection and the production of charcoal for energy (see Map 21).

Sources for map and commentary:

Campbell, David & David Hammond, *Floristic Inventory of Tropical Countries*, London: Friends of the Earth, 1989; Myers, Norman & Richard A. Houghton, 'Deforestation Rates in Tropical Forests, and Their Climatic Implications' (First Draft), London: Friends of the Earth, 1989; 'Paradise Lost?' London: EarthLife Foundation, 1986; World Resources Institute/International Institute for Environment and Development, *World Resources 1988-89*, New York: Basic Books, 1988.

6 DRINKING WATER

The World Health Organization defines reasonable access to safe drinking water in an urban area as 'access to piped water or a public standpipe within 200 metres of a dwelling'; for rural areas, the WHO definition of reasonable access is 'drinking water within 15 minutes walking distance'. Interpretation of these definitions, even in the definition of what is rural and what is urban, is clearly open to subjective judgement; variations in definition mean that comparisons between countries may be misleading. In general, much of the international data available on water provision must be accepted with scepticism.

In 1980, the United Nations launched the International Drinking Water Supply and Sanitation Decade in an effort to improve access to potable water and sanitation in developing countries. The mid-decade report showed promising signs for rural dwellers: worldwide, access to safe water had increased from 33 percent to 45 percent; the picture for the world's urban population had remained static: the worldwide average being about 75 percent. However, the report also noted that the per capita cost of providing water and sanitation services continued to increase despite the development of less expensive technologies, which suggests that governments may not be able to sustain improvements in water supply.

To support a reasonable quality of life requires approximately 80 litres of water per person per day. Around the world, average consumption ranges from 5.4 litres per day in Madagascar to more than 500 litres (approximately 160 US gallons) per day in the USA. Everywhere, demands on water are high, and growing fast. In the USA, it is estimated that household water consumption will quadruple between 1967 and 2000, and that the demands of industry will increase fivefold.

The main problems in relation to water supply vary between rich and poor countries, although sewage is polluting rivers everywhere (see Map 16). In poor countries, the greatest difficulty is the cost of bringing piped water to more people. In the rich world, there are growing problems of protecting water supplies from pollution. Groundwater and rivers are threatened by the use of pesticides and fertilizers in agriculture and by disposal methods for the increasing quantities of industrial and toxic waste produced by industry (see Maps 25 and 27). The UK Department of the Environment reported in 1988 that some drinking water sources had had to be 'abandoned because of pollution from landfill sites'. And in February 1990 the *Observer* reported that over 1300 landfill sites used for disposal of toxic waste were posing 'some risk' to water supplies.

Ideally, drinking water should come from unpolluted groundwater. However, this is an ideal in rapid retreat, and currently more than half the population of OECD countries and 70 percent of the US population drinks water that has been passed through waste water treatment plants. The danger in this is that not all waste can be removed in treatment, and the chemical agents used in treatment may themselves pose health risks.

Sources for maps and commentary:
Goldsmith, Edward & Nicholas Hildyard, eds., *The Earth Report*, London: Mitchell Beazley, 1988; Myers, Norman, ed., *Gaia: An Atlas of Planet Management*, London: Pan; New York: Doubleday, 1984; Lean, Geoffrey and Polly Ghazi, 'Britain's Buried Poison', *The Observer*, February 4, 1990; Organization for Economic Cooperation and Development (OECD), *OECD Environmental Data Compendium, 1989*, Paris: OECD, 1989; World Health Organization (WHO), International Drinking Supply and Sanitation Decade, *Review of National Progress 1983*, Geneva, 1986; WHO, *World Health Statistics Annual*, Geneva, 1986.

7 HUNGER AND PLENTY

The Hunger Report, an annual assessment of the state of hunger in the world, introduces the issue in this way: 'No one really knows how many hungry people there are in the world. No one knows the toll of hunger because hunger is difficult to define, because the statistical data are weak or nonexistent, and because efforts to improve data collection and analysis have been limited. But beyond these real difficulties, we may not know how many hungry people there are in the world because we may not want to know. To know how many hungry there are in a world of plenty is to measure the inadequacies of our economies to sustain all, of our societies to provide for all, and of our common humanity to care for all'.

It is by now commonplace to observe that there does exist more than enough food in the world to feed everyone adequately. Hunger reflects social derangement more than it reflects the capacity for food production.

Most international statistics on food and hunger measure the average availability of food supply, which is not the same as food consumption: because food is 'available' does not mean that everyone has access to it. Food consumption is mediated by class, gender, and age, among other variables. It is subject to serious disruption, most noticeably by war. Food supplies are often the intentional targets of armed conflict, which, not surprisingly, affects the poorest, hungriest, and most vulnerable in the population first, chief among whom are women and their dependent children.

The production and supply of food are obviously affected by environmental factors. Agendas for action on food and hunger have to tackle such issues as land erosion (see Map 11); increasing agro-chemical dependence (see Map 9); the need to conserve wild genes for the protection and maintenance of crops (see Map 10); and even the possibility of a changing world climate.

Sources for map and commentary:
Food and Agriculture Organization (FAO), *The State of Food and Agriculture*, 1989; FAO, *Production Statistics Yearbook*, Rome, 1987; Kates, Robert, et al, *The Hunger Report: 1988* and *Update: 1989*, Brown University: Alan Shawn Feinstein World Hunger Program, 1989.

8 LIVING OFF THE LAND

The proportion of people directly engaged in agriculture worldwide is dropping rapidly: in developing countries, from 70 percent in 1970 to 50 percent in 1990; in developed countries over the same period, from 16 percent to 8 percent. Meanwhile the number of people that each hectare of land must support is increasing dramatically. The amount of land available is relatively fixed, while the world's population is growing.

The race to obtain bigger crop yields out of a fixed agricultural base has been directed by large multinational chemical and agro-business enterprises. While all evidence shows that small farms are more efficient and productive than large farms, the worldwide trend is towards larger and larger consolidated agricultural holdings. Similarly, although food grown with heavy doses of chemicals is known to have a lower nutritional value, the 'drugging' of world agriculture continues (see Map 9). Finally, although land reform has proven to be the single most-effective means of increasing agricultural productivity, and despite recent revolutions waged on the promise of land reform, little is changing: in Peru, for example, 93% of all agricultural land is owned by the top 10% of landowners; in El Salvador, 78%; in Guatemala, 76%.

Much deforestation in Central and South America (see Map 5) is a direct consequence of distorted land tenure systems: huge areas of forest have single owners, who then assume the right to clear-cut forest to make way for large cattle-ranching enterprises. The cattle businesses themselves are often owned by foreign companies in conjunction with a country's largest landholders. Intervention in deforestation almost always brings environmentalists into direct conflict with the political and economic elite who own most of the land. In many countries, land reform and environmental reform must go hand in hand.

Sources for map and commentary:

Gramfors, Bo, *Concise Earth Atlas: The Book of Everything*, Stockholm: Esselte Map Service, 1989; Kurian, George, *The New Book of World Rankings*, New York: Facts on File, 1984; Food and Agriculture Organization (FAO), *Production Statistics Yearbook, 1988,* Rome: 1989.

9 CHEMICAL FIX

World agriculture is hooked on synthetic chemicals. The use of agro-chemicals has increased tenfold since World War II, and most crops are now grown with the assistance of artificial fertilizers and biocides. In 1988, for example, American farmers used almost 19 million tonnes of synthetic fertilizers and 255,000 tonnes of pesticides. The demand is for new and stronger chemicals, and for heavier doses. But chemical dependence is cyclical: fertilizers, which may appear to be the most benign of agro-chemicals, disrupt natural soil balance and crop ecology; this then encourages the use of herbicides, insecticides, and pesticides; these chemicals then strip soils of nutrients, which then necessitates heavier use of fertilizers.

Agricultural chemicals pose a grave pollution threat to entire ecosystems. Chemical runoff from croplands causes river eutrophication; insecticides and herbicides kill 'benign' animals and birds as well as 'pests'. DDT nearly wiped out dozens of domestic bird species on the eastern seaboard of the USA before its use was banned in the early 1970s; meanwhile in Thailand, DDT is now threatening drinking water supplies throughout the country; and over large regions of Central America, where pesticide use levels are among the highest in the world, wildlife is being decimated and the natural ecology is crumbling.

In addition to the indirect health threat of chemical residues remaining in food, agro-chemicals pose additional direct threats to human health. One person in the world dies from pesticide poisoning every two hours. In the USA, the Environmental Protection Agency estimates that at least 66 of the roughly 300 pesticide ingredients commonly used by farmers are 'probable carcinogens', and dozens more are known to cause birth defects, nervous system disorders, and other chronic illnesses. Accidents in the manufacture and storage of agro-chemicals have killed thousands of people worldwide and caused grave environmental damage. Many of the major industrial accidents over the past twenty years have involved agro-chemical production facilities: among the most prominent of these have been the accidents at Bhopal and Seveso plus the Basle chemical spill into the River Rhine (see Map 26).

Although agricultural chemicals are a known threat to the environment and to human health, the agro-chemical industry is very big business and the chemical lobby is powerful enough to evade or defeat most regulatory efforts. One favoured tactic of the industry is to shift production and markets when domestic regulation threatens chemical production. Current estimates suggest that 75 per cent of the pesticides used in the Third World would not be allowed in the USA, and many of the chemicals used by farmers in poorer countries are actually banned in first world markets, but produced by American and West European firms for overseas use. The USA exports more than 18 million kgs of DDT annually, but a clear example of the shift from home consumption to export is offered by British export figures for DDT. In 1980, British exports were 1840 kgs, yet in 1984, after the pesticide was banned for domestic use, exports rose to 125,503 kgs.

Fertilizer use is monitored closely by the United Nations' Food and Agriculture Organization (FAO). There is no comparable record of international pesticide manufacture and use; the best monitoring of this side of the chemical industry comes from independent environmental and consumer groups.

Sources for map and commentary:
Food and Agriculture Organization (FAO), *Fertilizer Yearbook 1988*, Rome, 1989; FAO, *Production Statistics Yearbook 1987*, Rome 1988; FAO, *Trade Statistics Yearbook 1988*, Rome 1989; Goldsmith, Edward & Nicholas Hildyard, eds., *The Earth Report*, London: Mitchell Beazley, 1988; Mercier, Michel & Morrell Draper, 'Chemical Safety: The International Outlook', *World Health*, August/Sept., 1984; Schneider, Keith, 'Pesticide Regulation: Slow and Unsteady,' *New York Times*, March 19, 1989; Weir, David & Mark Schapiro, *Circle of Poison*, Berkeley, CA: Institute for Food and Development Policy, 1981.

10 SHRINKING GENES

Genetic diversity is essential for the maintenance of ecological stability. Food plants that people have 'domesticated' do not endure on their own, isolated as they are from cross-fertilization with other genetically diverse plants. Most of the world's food now derives from about 20 plant species. Yet food crops must always be reinforced with infusions of genes from wild species. These wild relatives possess genes, for example, that protect against pests and disease, improve tolerance to drought and even improve nutritional values.

A number of cultivated crops have wild gene relatives found only in rainforest, which is being rapidly destroyed (see Map 5). The loss of this and other important plant habitat is one primary problem. So also is the spread of monoculture practised by large-scale agro-business, especially in industrial countries. This reliance on monoculture is itself destroying important wild plant genetic material. One observer has noted: 'The products of agro-technology are displacing the source upon which the technology is based. It is analogous to taking stones from the foundation to repair the roof.' The foundation of plant genetic diversity in the world is on the point of collapse.

Genetic material, or germplasm, can be collected and stored as seeds, plants, cuttings, pollen and/or tissue culture, depending on the species. Most of the critical areas for collection of wild genetic material so far identified are in the 'Third World'. However there are many less valuable sources that also need urgent attention and preservation. The identification of the genetic origins of plants is a herculean task, and one barely begun.

There is no such thing as self-sufficiency in plant resources. The International Board for Plant Genetic Resources (IBPGR) is supported by the United Nations and has taken global responsibility for the coordination of germplasm collection and storage. Most species now being collected and preserved by the IBPGR as priorities are cultivated crops. A number of international, mostly private, agencies are also engaged in collecting and preserving genetic material in gene banks.

Genetic engineering involves the deliberate manipulation of an organism's nucleic acid, or genes, to give it new properties. Genetic engineering has great potential for improving food production.

increasing resistance to disease and replacing 'defective genes'. However, it is possible for a genetically-engineered organism to escape the confines of a controlled experiment and become an opportunistic organism that could cause widespread disease and ecological disruption. The deliberate release of genetically-engineered organisms in field trials has been vigorously opposed, but releases are occurring at an increasing rate. Four releases of engineered organisms have occurred in countries other than those identified on the map.

Sources for map and commentary:
UK Department of the Environment, personal communication; Myers, Norman, ed., *Gaia: An Atlas of Planet Management*, London: Pan; New York: Doubleday, 1984; Prescott-Allen, R & C. Prescott-Allen, *Genes from the Wild*, London: Earthscan, 1988.

11 LOSING GROUND

Desertification was a big media issue of the 1970s and early 1980s. Described as a problem of over-exploitation of marginal lands in arid climates (especially in the Sahel area of Africa), the term conjured up images of 'deserts on the march'. Desertification has now taken on a low profile, replaced by newer global concerns such as ozone depletion and the greenhouse effect, and the concept itself has come under much critical review.

Nonetheless, soil loss - whether technically described as desertification or not - is still a pressing global concern. Soil loss is threatening agricultural viability on all six continents. In Australia, six tonnes of topsoil are eroded for every tonne of produce grown; in the USA, a third of all cropland is affected by erosion; over much of Asia, 40 percent of the land is at high risk of erosion or desertification.

Erosion - the removal of soil by wind or water - is a natural and ongoing process, but one that is dramatically aggravated and advanced by human activity, particularly the removal of vegetation. When forests are cut down or land is cleared for agriculture or animal grazing, there is nothing left to stabilize the soil, and rapid soil loss follows. In the late 1980s, the deadly landslides and floods that have plagued many Himalayan states, Bangladesh in particular, are largely attributed to the linked problems of deforestation and erosion.

Traditional peasant farming systems are often blamed for erosion problems. In fact, the greater problem is the spread of mechanized farming, the development of cash crops for export, and the introduction of vast livestock ranges that have led to overgrazing and unsustainably intensive agriculture.

Sources for map and commentary:
Goldsmith, Edward & Nicholas Hildyard, eds., *The Earth Report*, London: Mitchell Beazley, 1988; Myers, Norman, ed., *Gaia: An Atlas of Planet Management*, London: Pan; New York: Doubleday, 1984; United Nations Environment Programme (UNEP) *World Conservation Strategy*, 1980; World Resources Institute/Institute for Environment and Development, *World Resources 1988-89*, New York: Basic Books, 1988.

12 FISHING FOR FOOD

Fish is a major source of food for many in the world - fisheries supply 23 percent of the world's protein - and fishing provides a livelihood for millions of people. Since 1950, global yields of fish (both marine and fresh-water) have risen over fourfold, from 20 million tonnes to more than 85 million tonnes.

However, world fish stocks are now threatened by many factors, including over-exploitation, pollution, (see, for example, Map 22) and wetlands destruction (see Map 14). After some years of increasing yields, the stocks of many fisheries are declining precipitously. According to a mid-1980s survey by the United Nations' Food and Agriculture Organization (FAO), 11 major ocean fishing grounds, including some newly exploited grounds, are now overfished to the point of collapse. Given the greater dependence on fish for food in Third World countries, it is the poor who will be suffering first and most as fisheries decline.

Statistics monitoring the state of fisheries are often contradictory, and usually considerably out of date. Estimates of catches are highly unreliable and even the most reliable figures, from FAO, must be treated with some caution. In most statistical summaries, 'artisanal' fishing and small coastal independent fishing enterprises are often overlooked, although these supply much of the demand for fish in poorer countries.

Sources for map and commentary:
Food and Agriculture Organization (FAO), *World Food Report*, Rome, 1985; FAO, *Fishery Statistics*, 1986, 1987; Myers, Norman, ed., *Gaia: An Atlas of Planet Management*, London: Pan; New York: Doubleday, 1984.

13 CITY SPRAWL

Cities have always acted as focal points in the development of nation-states, and as symbols of opportunity in the popular imagination. They remain symbolically powerful, but the reality of urbanization is rapidly changing. Some cities remain small in scale and functionally intact. But as other cities — the 'hotspots' on this map, as well as others unnamed — grow into vast conglomerations, they are both uncontrollable and unsustainable. Governments cannot afford to provide the vast infrastructure that is needed to accommodate adequately the huge numbers of people drawn to city life.

In consequence, the social structure of 'mega-cities' around the world is increasingly bifurcated into a small, powerful, and often extremely wealthy elite class, and a huge underclass that is ill-housed or homeless, ill-fed, and unserved by even basic municipal services. There is no poverty more squalid than urban poverty, and in the rapidly urbanizing centres of the world, city life and poverty seem synonymous. Most of the people migrating to the largest and fastest-growing cities in the world today will end up living in shanty-towns, slums or 'cardboard cities' on the outskirts, with no running water, sanitation services or health services. Many will end up with work as street vendors, as exploitatively-paid piece-workers or, especially many young women, as prostitutes or domestic servants for the wealthy.

Many of today's new urban arrivals are unwilling migrants, people displaced from their rural landholdings by war, famine, massive 'development' schemes such as large dams (see Map 20), and agricultural 'modernization'. For others, willing migrants, the attractions of the city are not diminished by the reality of urban poverty: cities still offer the possibility of economic opportunities not found elsewhere, the hope of greater social, political or religious freedom, and amenities not possible in rural settings.

The locus of global urbanization is shifting. In 1960, six out of ten of the world's largest cities were in industrialized countries: New York, Los Angeles, London, the Rhine/Ruhr conglomeration, Paris, and Moscow. By the year 2000, only two cities in the industrial world, New York and Tokyo, will remain in the top ten ranking. Mexico City, ranked 15 in size in 1960, will be the world's largest city by the year 2000.

As cities grow, in absolute size and proportional importance, they play a larger part in shaping the global environment. Under the pressure of urban sprawl, agricultural land is paved over, wetlands are drained, natural habitats are destroyed, rivers are diverted, and wildlife habitats are pushed further and further into the margins. The internal ecology of cities also changes: pollutants of all kinds are concentrated in urban centres, and many cities have become highly hazardous places to live. Environmental action must acknowledge the global nature of the urban problem. Efforts must be made to make cities more humane places to live - and more environmentally benign.

Sources for map and commentary:
Atlas de Carreteras Mexico, Mexico City, Guia Roji, 1987; McDowell, Bert, 'Mexico City: An Alarming Giant', *National Geographic*, August 1984; United Nations, Department of International Economic and Social Affairs, *The Prospects of World Urbanization*, 1987; United Nations, *Compendium of Human Settlement Statistics*, 1983.

14 COASTAL CRISIS

Wetlands fringe most coastlines of the world, as mangroves in the tropics and subtropics, and as salt marshes in the temperate zones. They mediate between the ecosystems of land and sea, serving as huge reservoirs of species diversity, providing rich wildlife habitats for birds, animals, and fish. They provide the spawning grounds for most of the world's commercial fisheries, they act as natural buffers that temper the effects of extreme flooding and drought, they filter pollutants out of maritime systems, they recharge groundwater drinking supplies, and they stabilize coastal erosion. They stabilize and support the health of the planet.

Wetlands are under extreme threat almost everywhere in the world. Clear-cutting is perhaps the greatest single threat, but pollution and urban development rank close behind. Urban development alone has claimed almost half the wetlands in the USA, and in California and Iowa, more than 90 percent. South-East Asia has the largest mangrove ecosystem in the world, but it is rapidly being clear-cut by commercial logging operations, especially in Malaysia, Indonesia, and Bangladesh.

Like many other environmental problems, but especially so, the world's wetlands need international cooperation for their protection. The significance of wetlands, and the consequences of their loss, cannot be contained by national borders. The migrating birds of Western Europe, for example, depend on wetlands in northern Africa for refuge on their journey; the drainage of wetlands in Louisiana threatens the fisheries of the entire Gulf of Mexico.

Since 1971, some measure of international wetlands protection has been offered through the Convention on Wetlands of International Significance (also known as the 'Ramsar Convention'), but this convention is ratified by only 43 countries, and while 77,000 square miles of wetlands have fallen under its statutory protection, this represents less than 2 percent of the world's wetland areas.

Sources for map and commentary:

Chapman, V.J., *Ecosystems of the World and Wet Coastal Ecosystems*, New York: Elsevier, 1977; Conservation Foundation, *State of the Environment: A View Toward the Nineties*, Washington DC, 1987; Houck, Oliver, 'America's Mad Dash to the Sea,' *The Amicus Journal*, Summer 1988; 'Mangroves: An Ecosystem in Danger', *Ambio*, vol. 9, 1980; Saenger, P., E.J. Hegerl & J.D.S. Davie, *Global Status of Mangrove Ecosystems*, IUCN (Cambridge) Commission on Ecology Papers no. 3, 1983.

15 WASTE

International information on levels of municipal and household waste generation, most experts agree, is little more than an educated guess, although some general points are clear: worldwide generation of waste appears to amount to about one billion tonnes per year, and is growing rapidly; the biggest waste producers are rich countries and, within poor countries, rich people. Affluence produces effluence, literally.

There is also a significant difference in the kind of garbage thrown away by rich and poor: in rich countries, glass, paper, metals and other durables constitute a larger share of garbage than in poor countries, where more of the waste is organic material. This difference has important implications for waste disposal: organic garbage can be composted, which is the safest method of waste disposal, whereas other materials are less easily disposed of. Plastics are the least disposable of any garbage, yet the proportion of plastics in garbage is increasing dramatically. In 1987, the USA alone produced 26 billion kgs. of plastics; by volume, plastics now represent about 30 percent of the US waste stream.

At the beginning of the 1990s, most garbage in most places in the world is dumped in landfills. But cities and countries everywhere are running out of landfill space. Given the landfill crisis, attention is turning to incineration (optimistically called, by those in the industry, 'waste to energy' disposal). Incineration is a high-cost means of waste treatment that generates air pollution and leaves a highly toxic residue that itself then needs disposal. A number of countries, including Belgium, France, West Germany, and the UK, burn some of their waste at sea on incinerator ships, although the international community is moving closer to banning this highly polluting and very dangerous practice. Other countries simply dump their municipal garbage at sea. Although this practice, too, is being phased out, we will live with its legacy for years to come, in the form of increasing epidemics of marine mammal illnesses, and increasing incidents, some of which are already recorded in Western Europe and the USA, of deep-sea trash washing up on beaches.

Recycling, which is a cheap, revenue-generating, and low-technology solution, is slowly gaining favour in most industrialized countries, but still faces heavy competition from incineration. In poor countries, recycling has always ranked high in waste reduction, and whole communities of people in most Third World cities support themselves as dump-scavengers and recyclers.

The waste crisis has sparked interest among rich countries in the possibilities of an international waste trade. With no room in their own backyards, states and industries in the developed world are scanning the globe for countries poor enough to want to accept municipal trash for (usually low) dumping fees. (See Map 27 for a parallel trade in toxic waste). In 1989, an American waste disposal firm closed a deal to dump thousands of tonnes of US household waste on a Pacific atoll in the Marshall Islands. It is a great irony that one of the selling points for the deal was that the garbage could provide landfill for the low-lying Marshalls, which would otherwise be vulnerable to flooding if sea levels rise as a result of global warming.

Sources for map and commentary:
Cointreau, Sandra, *Solid Waste Recycling: Case Studies in Developing Countries*, Washington DC: World Bank, 1987; Levenson, Howard, Office of Technology Assessment, US Congress, personal communication; Organization for Economic Cooperation and Development (OECD), *OECD Environmental Data Compendium, 1989*, Paris: OECD, 1989; World Resources Institute/Institute for Environment and Development, *World Resources 1988-89*, New York: Basic Books, 1988; World Action on Recycling Materials for Energy from Rubbish (WARMER), Tunbridge Wells, personal communication; Worldwatch Institute, *State of the World: 1989*, New York: Norton, 1989.

16 SEWAGE

In heavily populated areas, especially the rapidly-growing urban conglomerations of poorer countries, sewage pollution is a primary cause of the worldwide trend in deterioration of water quality. In developing countries, most municipal sewage receives little or no treatment, and separation of drinking water from sewage disposal is inadequate; sewage contamination of drinking water is a major factor in the high rates of infant mortality and morbidity recorded in many poorer countries, much of which is caused by gastro-intestinal infections.

In older industrial areas, municipal water and sewage facilities, many built in the last century, are overwhelmed by population pressures, and a decline in investment in sewage disposal in the late 1970s and early 1980s has resulted in the downgrading of river water quality in most urban areas. Until recently, sewage in most industrialized countries was dumped directly into the nearest body of water: for example, until the mid-1960s, American and Canadian cities pumped untreated sewage directly into the Great Lakes, contributing to its reputation as one of the most polluted bodies of water in the world. In most cases, it was not municipal farsightedness but agitation by independent environmental groups that led to pressure for sewage treatment and an end to direct dumping. Efforts to clean up urban waterways, now underway in many industrialized cities, are estimated to cost billions of dollars.

The accuracy of statistics that measure the provision of sanitation facilities is widely suspect. International compendiums typically provide dramatically different figures: for example, while the World Health Organization reports adequate sanitation provisions for 40 percent of Uganda's urban population in the mid-1980s, an independent development agency reports only 20 percent coverage. In some cases, statistics may be manipulated to serve political agendas that might be undercut by reports of low levels of public health services provision. These statistical variations, often dramatic or confusing, suggest the difficulties inherent in attempts to monitor public and environmental wellbeing on a global basis.

Sources for map and commentary:
Organization for Economic Cooperation and Development (OECD), *OECD Environmental Data Compendium, 1989,* Paris: OECD, 1989; United Nations Environment Programme (UNEP), *Environmental Data Report,* 2nd ed. 1989-90, Oxford: Blackwell, 1989; World Health Organization (WHO), *World Health Statistics Annual,* 1986; World Resources Institute/Institute for Environment and Development, *World Resources 1988-89,* New York: Basic Books, 1988.

17 AIR QUALITY

This map depicts urban levels of three major air pollutants - sulphur dioxides, nitrogen oxides, and particulates ('dust and dirt'). Ninety percent of anthropogenic sulphur dioxide emissions are from the burning of certain fossil fuels; nitrogen oxides come primarily from car and truck emissions; and particulates from both cars and fossil fuel combustion. All three contribute to a range of respiratory illnesses, including bronchitis, pneumonia, asthma and lung cancer, although the health effects vary with the intensity and duration of exposures. Both sulphur dioxide and nitrogen oxides are major components of acid rain and nitrogen oxides are also a minor greenhouse gas.

Measuring air quality is a precise science that must, by its nature, be carried out under imprecise and unpredictable conditions. Standardized international measurements are only available for a scattering of cities, and drawing comparisons from city data is difficult because of wide variations in place, time and the frequency of air monitoring samples. Sometimes, indeed, monitoring is only carried out at sites where there is a known severe problem. This leads to a bias towards sampling cities with higher concentrations of pollutants. Despite these caveats, though, it is still possible to make certain generalizations about air quality problems in the world's cities.

The air in most cities is in fact a chemical soup of dozens of pollutants. There are a number of others beyond the three pollutants illustrated on the map. Carbon monoxide, largely the product of car emissions, is one of the mostly widely distributed urban air pollutants, but there is no available international data set measuring its levels. Similarly, ozone, also known as 'photochemical smog', is a serious air quality concern in many cities, but again there are no worldwide statistics. Los Angeles is still the city with the greatest ozone problem in the world. Ozone was originally believed to be a problem peculiar to Los Angeles, because of its special topography and high density of cars, but photochemical smog is now known to occur in and downwind of most major cities in the world. Dublin also has a serious smog problem - but in this case, the smog is from the 350,000 tonnes of coal burned in the city's households each year.

Most urban air pollutant levels are increasing, largely because of increases in the numbers of cars and trucks (see Map 31). There are some broad estimates of the costs involved in reducing air pollutant levels: that to cut sulphur dioxide emissions in half in the USA would cost an estimated US$5 billion a year; to halve sulphur emissions in the EEC would cost from US$5 billion to US$7 billion per year. It is even more difficult to quantify the real costs of existing air pollution, but one EEC estimate gives US$13 billion for loss of fisheries, crops, forests, and health.

Sources for map and commentary:
Global Environment Monitoring System (GEMS), *Assessment of Urban Air Quality,* Nairobi: UNEP/WHO, 1988; 'Monitoring the Global Environment: An Assessment of Urban Air Quality.' Special Issue report. *Environment,* October 1989; Organization for Economic Cooperation and Development (OECD), *OECD Environmental Data Compendium,* 1989, Paris: OECD, 1989; World Health Organization (WHO), *Air Quality Guidelines for Europe,* Copenhagen: 1987; World Commission on Environment and Development, *Our Common Future,* Oxford: Oxford University Press, 1987; World Resources Institute/International Institute for Environment and Development, *World Resources 1988-89,* New York: Basic Books, 1988.

18 ENERGY BUDGETS

Energy production and consumption are closely monitored, both by government agencies and private industry, and statistics on international use are widely available, if sometimes highly technical. As always, information on commercially-traded commodities, such as oil or coal, is much more reliable than is information on fuels of local reliance, such as firewood and small-scale hydropower. Firewood, the largest biomass energy source, and other biomass fuels together provide approximately 14 percent of the world's energy.

The USA is by far the largest consumer of commercial energy, but a number of other countries in Western Europe have comparable per capita consumption levels. Current global energy consumption rates are increasing on an average of 3 percent per year, the largest share of which is in the industrialized world. Overall, it would appear that the pace of growth in consumption is somewhat lessening, but consumption rates often fluctuate considerably over the short term.

Energy consumption provides a measure of our impact on ecological systems. The production, extraction and use of coal, oil, gas, and nuclear power, which power much of the world, all have destructive environmental consequences (see Maps 17, 22 and 23). The renewable energy sources most widely used, hydro power and firewood, are more environmentally benign, but are not unproblematic (see Maps 20 and 21). Firewood is in increasingly short supply, and even though it provides the sole energy source for many 'third world' households, it may not continue to be a viable energy source far into the next century.

Given this array of poor choices, energy conservation is crucial to the long-term viability of the planet. After the oil crisis of 1973, systematic efforts were made throughout the industrial world to increase energy efficiency, with impressive results: in the USA, cars will now travel 29 percent farther on a gallon of gasoline than they did in 1973; Denmark was able to reduce its total use of direct fuels by 20 percent between 1976 and 1980. The reasons to reduce energy consumption are now different but they are even more compelling.

Some would argue that conservation is necessary but not sufficient, and that we must radically alter our industries and economies to incorporate large-scale use of solar, geothermal, and wind energy sources, which hold the promise of being both renewable and non-polluting. Others see them as introducing environmental problems of their own. As yet, however, these technologies have received little support or interest, nor have they made much of a dent in traditional energy budgets.

Sources for map and commentary:

Conservation Foundation, *State of the Environment: A View Toward the Nineties*, Washington DC, 1987; Goldsmith, Edward & Nicholas Hildyard, eds., *The Earth Report*, London: Mitchell Beazley, 1988; United Nations, *Energy Statistics Yearbook 1987*, 1989; US Department of Energy, Energy Information Administration (EIA), *International Energy Annual, 1988*, Washington DC: DOE, 1989.

19 THE NUCLEAR FAMILY

Electricity generation by nuclear power began in 1955 with a small reactor in the Soviet Union. Since then, the growth of the industry has been dramatic. There are currently 421 operating nuclear power plants in the world, and another 144 reactors planned or under construction. In addition to the 32 countries with operating power plants, another 27 have some form of nuclear facility. Though the industry is widely perceived to have fundamental problems, there are actually few signs of its demise.

The USA is the world's largest exporter of nuclear technology, followed by the USSR; it is not coincidental that these two countries are also the world's largest military powers, and the world's largest military exporters. Military nuclear agendas and commercial nuclear programmes are closely intertwined. Any nuclear power reactor can be used to produce plutonium for bombs. Some, like 'fast breeder' reactors, are designed specifically to produce plutonium; others produce it as a by-product; many reactors are used for both weapons and energy production. Whether governments choose to acknowledge the interconnectedness of the military and civilian uses of nuclear programmes depends largely on domestic politics and international approbation.

The link between civilian nuclear power and military nuclear capability is made through the nuclear fuel cycle. To be able to make a nuclear weapon, a country has to have access to all five stages of the nuclear cycle, from uranium production through fuel reprocessing. Thus, South Korea, **111** which is technically striving for independence in its nuclear power capabilities, has no enrichment or reprocessing facilities; on the other hand, Argentina, which does not produce much power through nuclear facilities, has completed the fuel cycle. The fuel cycle also brings countries into the nuclear family even if they are not producing nuclear energy: Iraq, for example, has a nuclear fuel fabrication plant and Gabon mines uranium.

Spokespeople for the nuclear industry are quick to point out that nuclear power plants emit none of the greenhouse gases produced by oil and coal. This, however, is a dubious virtue, given that the operation of nuclear plants represents an ongoing public safety and health threat, and given the large volumes of highly toxic waste generated by the nuclear industry. Over the next 30 years, more than 25,000 cubic metres of high level waste will be generated by the top ten nuclear countries alone. There is literally no place to safely dispose of radioactive waste, and there are fewer and fewer places to store it. Until 1983, Belgium, the Netherlands, Switzerland and the UK dumped low-level radioactive waste at sea. This practice was halted by an international moratorium under the London Dumping Convention, an agreement consistently opposed by the British government. With the ban on ocean disposal, there is also no place, any more, to dispose of low-level radioactive waste. Most nuclear states are building up huge stockpiles of nuclear waste that no one wants and no one knows how to get rid of.

The nuclear accident at Chernobyl in 1986 provided powerful evidence that nuclear disasters transcend state borders and undermined support for nuclear power throughout Europe. Polls showed that opposition to nuclear power in the UK jumped frpm 70% before Chernobyl, to 85% after the accident; in Austria, opposition increased from 50% to 75%; in France, from 40% to 50%. In a national referendum in 1987, Italians voted to shut down permanently their nuclear power plants, although as of early 1990, it appeared that one plant was still operating.

Sources for map and commentary:

Commission of the European Communities, *The State of the Environment in the European Community, 1986*, Brussels, 1988; International Atomic Energy Agency *Annual Report for 1988*, Vienna: IAEA, 1989; 'The World's Nuclear Fuel Cycle Facilities', *Nuclear Engineering International*, December 1987; 'World List of Nuclear Power Plants', *Nuclear News*, August 1989.

20 HYDRO POWER

In 1950, there were about 5000 large dams in the world; thirty years later, by the early 1980s, there were 35,000 large dams, 53 percent of which were in China. The frenzy of dam construction appears to have now slowed worldwide, and in China in particular - in large measure because of environmental concerns.

Hydro power (which accounts for about 6 percent of worldwide energy use) is in itself a relatively cheap, renewable and non-polluting energy source. However the dams built to produce it present a number of serious environmental problems. The reservoirs for large dams are created by flooding vast swathes of land, often inundating valuable forest area, wildlife habitat or wetlands - often entire ecological communities. In warm climates, reservoirs can pose health hazards, increasing the incidence of waterborne disease, such as schistosomiasis, and 'river blindness'. The quality of water from dams often deteriorates, due to a build-up of salts and chemicals, posing threate to irrigated crops and drinking water supplies.

The construction of a large dam is a huge undertaking. Many of the largest dam projects in the world are funded with assistance from international aid agencies, most notably the World Bank. The twin Sadar Sarovar and Narmada Sagar dam projects in India, for example, estimated to displace 70,000 people by submerging 438 villages, was started with a US$450 million loan from the World Bank; it has become one of their most controversial projects. If the World Bank honours its recent commitment to phase out support for environmentally destructive projects, many of the largest dam projects now planned around the world will be halted. Local environmental pressure is also halting work on some large dams (see Map 37). Plans for a major dam on the Danube at Nagymaros, Hungary, were scrapped in 1988. In 1990, French environmentalists are fighting proposals for four large dams on the Loire, France's longest river. They have had some success. Two dams have already been cancelled and the battle continues.

The definition of 'large' dams, as agreed by international engineering associations, includes dams from 15 metres in height to 'mega' dams over 200 metres high. Statistics on hydro power, and on dams, are readily available from 'pro-dam' sources, mainly detailed records of dam characteristics and construction, and from 'anti-dam' groups who monitor the environmental and social costs of dams.

Sources for map and commentary:
International Commission on Large Dams, *World Register of Dams*, Paris: 1984; International Rivers Network, *World Rivers Review*, July/August, 1989; Mermel, T.W., 'The World's Major Dams and Hydro Plants', *International Water Power and Dam Construction*, vol. 41, 1989; Parcels, S. & T.B. Stoel, 'The Large Dam Controversy', Unpublished draft for the World Bank, 1989; Probe International, 'Water Projects With World Bank Involvement', *World Rivers Review*, September/October 1989; Simons, M., 'Brazil Wants its Dams, But at What Cost?' *New York Times*, March 12, 1989.

21 FIREWOOD

Firewood is a local, self-reliant energy source. Since most statistical information is collected on a national or even international level, information on the supply and use of firewood is partial, inconsistent, and often based on very small samples. Official reports also invariably underestimate rural fuelwood use.

Within a single country there is often considerable variation in firewood provision – variations lost in national summaries. Information on the amount of time spent collecting firewood – always women's work -- must be treated with a good deal of caution. The data we provide on this subject is based on a small sample of communities and cannot be assumed to represent a general or national average.

Nonetheless, the general situation in relation to firewood is clear. Many people in many 'third world' countries rely entirely on firewood for energy, cooking, and warmth. About 70 - 95 percent of all firewood is used for rural domestic purposes, and the remainder is used in cottage industries and small-scale commercial enterprises. Almost everywhere in the world, firewood is becoming scarce, and the effort to collect it is taking a larger and larger share of the working day. Many women in rural areas report that they are now spending so much time collecting firewood that they have little time for other activities, such as growing and cooking food. With less time to prepare food, simpler diets are being adopted – in the Sahel, for example, many women have shifted from cooking millet to rice. Nutrition suffers even before a full firewood crisis arises.

The firewood shortage has been precipitated by a number of converging factors. Everywhere in the world, deforestation for commercial logging or agriculture is the primary cause of local firewood scarcity. In addition, though, urban demand is putting pressure on rural resources. Firewood for Delhi, for example, comes from Madhya Pradesh, 700 kilometres away, and requires clear-felling of 6 hectares of forest a day. Whereas fuelwood for rural uses is often twigs and fallen branches, commercial users will cut down an entire tree – representing the difference between sustainable tree use and deforestation.

Sources for map and commentary:
Agarwal, Bina, *Cold Hearths and Barren Slopes: The Fuelwood Crisis in the Third World*, Riverdale, MD: Riverdale Press, 1986; Food and Agriculture Organization (FAO), *Map of the Fuelwood Situation in the Developing Countries*, Rome: FAO, 1981; FAO, *Yearbook of Forest Products, 1982, 1984*; Richard Hosier, University of Pennsylvania, personal communication; Smil, V. & W.E. Knowland, eds., *Energy in the Developing World: The Real Energy Crisis*, Oxford: Oxford University Press, 1980; United Nations Environment Programme (UNEP), *Environmental Data Report*, 2nd ed. 1989-90, Oxford: Blackwell, 1989; United Nations Statistical Office, *Energy Statistics Yearbook 1985,1987* and *Energy Statistics Yearbook 1986*, 1988.

22 OIL POLLUTION

The economy – and lifestyle – of the industrialized world is entirely dependent on oil. Oil is big business, both for private and public enterprise and state revenue: Exxon, the world's largest oil company made a net profit of US$5 billion in 1987; 55 states depend essentially on a single product for their export income – for 24 of them, that product is oil and gas. The oil industry seems larger than life; so, unfortunately, is the pollution it causes. The extraction and transport of oil are among the highest-risk industrial activities, causing long-lasting ecological disruption and widespread pollution.

More than 6 million metric tonnes of oil are released into the world's oceans each year; roughly 1 tonne is spilled for every 1000 tonnes extracted. Marine tanker accidents are not the largest source of oil pollution, but they are often the most dangerous, releasing large amounts of oil in a short period of time, often close to shore. The threat posed by single acute oil spills has increased over the past twenty years, as oil companies have switched to larger and larger vessels in an effort to cut costs. Today's supertankers average twice the size and carry ten times the amount of oil as tankers that worked the oil routes twenty years ago.

The chronic release of oil from maritime shipping operations represents an even greater environmental problem than acute spills. On oil supply routes, for example, oil tankers routinely flush out their tanks with sea water on the return trip, in so doing releasing thousands of tonnes of oil annually. Oily trails around the world mark the major shipping routes.

When accidental maritime oil spills do happen, as they do on an average of three a day worldwide, legal and financial responsibility for the ensuing pollution is often difficult to assign. Many oil companies register their ships under 'flags of convenience' in such countries as Liberia, the Bahamas, Cyprus or Panama. These 'open registries' allow companies to run ships with lower-cost, non-union crews, to evade certain corporation taxes, and to avoid some national and international regulations. Registries of convenience also obscure the trail of corporate responsibility for accidents and spills.

In mapping the distribution of oil spills, our original intention had been to allocate responsibility to individual oil companies. This proved to be impossible. Despite the volumes of data kept by tanker associations, oil associations, and maritime associations, no one, it appears, monitors oil spills by company – or, if such records do exist, they are not open to public scrutiny. This gap reinforces the sense that oil accidents 'just happen', somehow without human agency. It is even difficult to establish, in the first place, the occurrence of spills. Unless they are spectacular accidents, most domestic media coverage ignores spills that occur elsewhere in the world, and most small spills in domestic waters are not newsworthy. The data used here is a compilation from dozens of sources, and yet we know the information to be still incomplete.

A primary argument against increased use of renewable energy sources, such as solar power, is its cost. It is argued that conventional sources of energy, such as oil, are much cheaper. However, the true cost of oil is mostly hidden. The real tally of the cost of our oil dependency should include the cost of environmental damage and clean-ups. It should also include expenditure on military forces used to 'secure' oil supply routes and oil production regions; oil company subsidies and tax allowances, and the cost of the trade deficits that most oil-dependent nations now face.

Sources for map and commentary:
Couper, A., ed., *The Times Atlas of the Oceans*, London: Times Books; New York: Van Nostrand, 1983; International Tanker Owners' Pollution Federation (ITOPF), 'Spills over 5000 barrels,' mimeograph document; Levy, Eric, 'Oil Pollution in the World's Oceans,' *Ambio*, vol. 13, no. 4, 1984; McKenzie, Arthur, *Guide to the Selection of Tankers*, New York: Tanker Advisory Center, 1989; other Tanker Advisory Center publications; National Academy of Sciences (NAS), *Oil in the Sea: Inputs, Fates and Effects*, Washington DC: NAS, 1985; Organization for Economic Cooperation and Development (OECD), *OECD Environmental Data Compendium, 1989*, Paris: OECD, 1989; Starr, Gary & Susan Bryer Starr, 'The True Cost of Oil,' *Earth Island Journal*, Summer 1988.

23 FOSSIL FUEL POLLUTION

Fossil fuels are oil, gas and coal. Most industrial economies are entirely fossil-fuel dependent. The price of this dependency is severe pollution and, looming, the possible onset of global warming. The burning of fossil fuels produces a number of pollutants, including sulphur dioxide, nitrogen oxides, particulates (dirt and dust) and carbon monoxide.

The most serious fossil fuel pollutant is carbon dioxide. This is not in itself toxic, but in conjunction with other gases is the primary greenhouse gas (see Map 1). Most carbon dioxide in the atmosphere stems from burning fossil fuels. Worldwide releases from carbon dioxide from fossil fuel combustion currently amount to 22 billion tonnes per year. Other human activities that produce carbon dioxide include tropical forest destruction (see Map 5), cement production and natural gas burn-off flares. Smaller quantities are produced from natural sources, such as volcanoes and animal respiration.

Most fossil fuel pollution comes from a handful of rich, industrial countries. Canada and the USA produce, between them, 33 million tonnes of carbon dioxide a year. Carbon dioxide pollution is a pollution of privilege; but as is often the case in environmental concerns, the consequences and costs are borne globally.

Attempts to curb the problem are being thwarted by the very countries most responsible. In autumn 1989, 65 countries sponsored an international resolution to cut carbon dioxide emissions in industrial countries. It was defeated by objections from Japan, the USA and the USSR. The US and Japanese governments urged postponing action for 'further study', while USSR and other East European representatives opposed pollution limits claiming they could not afford them. In the countries creating most pollution, the adoption of carbon dioxide limits would probably require more fuel-efficient cars, more fuel-efficient electricity and extensive tree planting.

The other pollutants included on this map, sulphur dioxide and nitrogen oxides, are both major contributors to acid rain (see Map 24). Again, the primary sources of these pollutants are in the industrialized world and acid rain is a particular problem for Western Europe. Most West European governments, the UK being a notable exception, have joined together to form a '30% Club'. This commits them to reducing sulphur dioxide emissions by 30 percent by 1993 – not just by cutting back on fossil fuel use, but by persuading industry to devise less polluting techniques.

Sources for map and commentary:
Eliasson, Anton, et al, *Estimates of Airborne Transboundary Transport of Sulphur and Nitrogen over Europe*, Norwegian Meteorological Institute, 1988; Global Environment Monitoring System (GEMS), *Assessment of Urban Air Quality*, Nairobi: UNEP/WHO, 1988; Goldsmith, Edward & Nicholas Hildyard, eds., *The Earth Report*, London: Mitchell Beazley, 1988; Montgomery, Paul, 'US, Japan and Soviets Prevent Accord to Limit Carbon Dioxide', *New York Times*, November 8, 1989; Oak Ridge National Laboratory, *Estimates of CO2 Emissions from Fossil Fuel Burning and Cement Manufacturing*, Environmental Sciences Division Publication no. 3176, 1989.

24 ACID RAIN

The term 'acid rain' includes both the wet deposition of acidic sleet, snow, fog or rain and the dry deposition of nitrates and sulphates as they settle. Since the industrial revolution the chemical balance of the atmosphere has changed and acidification is being increased. This is mainly through the release of a very large additional burden of sulphur dioxide and nitrogen oxides from burning fossil fuels, notably coal in power stations and oil in motor vehicles (see Maps 23 and 31).

The acidity of a solution is measured in terms of 'pH'; pH1 is strongly acid, pH14 strongly alkaline, and pH7 is neutral. Weak acids such as lemon juice or vinegar have a pH of 3 to 4. Natural rainfall is usually slightly acid and has a pH of 6 to 7. On the map, 'high' acid rain pollution corresponds to an average rainfall pH of 4.9 to 5.1, 'very high' to pH4.5 – 4.7, and 'extremely high' to pH4.2 – 4.3.

Acid rain spares little. It erodes railway tracks; it corrodes the masonry of historic buildings and public statues. It causes natural ecosystems to crumble, destroying forests, crops and fish life in **115** lakes. To date, acid rain is doing the greatest damage in Europe. In southern Norway, 80 percent of the lakes and streams are technically 'dead'; 64 percent of UK forest is showing signs of acid rain damage; in central Switzerland, more than 40 per cent of conifer forest is dead or severely damaged.

Acid rain is, by definition, a trans-national problem – it shows no regard for state boundaries. Acid deposition has been a contentious issue between Canada and the USA for years; most acid deposition in Scandinavia is from other countries, coming downwind from Europe's major industrial centres.

Solutions to the acid rain problem are energy conservation, a shift to less polluting forms of transport, and the fitting of special equipment to reduce acid gas emissions: 'flue gas desulphurization' at power stations and three-way catalytic converters on motor vehicles. In 1985, 19 countries agreed to reduce sulphur emissions by a further 30 percent, but scientists estimate that the reduction must be very much higher if the lakes and forests of Scandinavia are to be saved from further damage.

Sources for map and commentary:

Goldsmith, Edward & Nicholas Hildyard, eds., *The Earth Report*, London, Mitchell Beazley, 1988; McCormick, John, *Acid Earth*, London: Earthscan, 1989; United Nations Environment Programme (UNEP), *Forest Damage and Air Pollution*, 1988; World Resources Institute/International Institute for Environment and Development, *World Resources 1988-89*, New York: Basic Books, 1988.

25 INDUSTRIAL WASTE

Industrial activity generates millions of tonnes of waste annually, much of it extremely toxic. Nowhere in the world are there effective constraints or regulations to control this practice, and the decision-makers in industry seem largely unwilling to police themselves. Industry likes to conduct 'business as usual' and the typical response is to fight tooth and nail against the demands of clean air legislation, chemical regulation, water quality standards, automobile emission standards, workplace health regulations, and any other legislation designed to protect our environment. In state-controlled economies, where the state and industry are one, there are even fewer opportunities for independent monitoring or control of industrial pollution.

Some 350 million tonnes of hazardous industrial wastes are generated worldwide each year, about 90 percent of which comes from industrial countries. The US Environmental Protection Agency has identified a top-priority national list of over 5000 hazardous sites ('Superfund sites') left behind by industry, which, together will cost billions of dollars to clean up. As the curtain of secrecy lifts from Eastern Europe, tales of dead rivers, unbreathable air, villages abandoned because of extreme pollution, and other industrial horrors are being revealed daily.

There are no good ways of getting rid of hazardous waste. In the UK, 82 percent of hazardous industrial waste is dumped in landfills (see commentary to Map 6). At the beginning of the 1990s, the UK was still dumping 8 percent of its hazardous waste at sea. Protests from other EEC countries and from environmentalists mean that this practice is to be phased out. In the USA, incineration is increasingly favoured by industry, but this creates other forms of pollution.

Detailed information on the extent, nature, and origin of industrial pollution is patchy: there are powerful forces at work to ensure that much of it remains unidentified. The 'blighted zones' identified on this map represent the most extreme cases of industrial pollution; literally thousands more zones of local blight scar every industrial country.

Sources for map and commentary:

Bellini, James, *High Tech Holocaust*, San Francisco: Sierra Club Books, 1986; National Wildlife Federation, *The Toxic 500*, 1987, New York: NWF, 1989; press reports; United Nations Environment Programme (UNEP), *Environmental Data Report*, 2nd ed. 1989-90, Oxford: Blackwell, 1989.

26 DEADLY INDUSTRY

This map identifies the major accidents of the past twenty years that have occurred during the manufacture and transport of hazardous industrial products. It does not include accidents that occur in their end-use and application. There are several biases in the data. More is known about accidents in the 'developed' world and, by definition, the focus is on acute events rather than chronic releases (see Map 25). Then there is a general absence of accidents involving weapons factories, military research laboratories and other military installations because of a dearth of information.

Industrial accidents involving the release of hazardous substances are a daily occurrence. But the record-keeping of these releases is entirely inadequate. Only large and spectacular accidents, such as the explosion of gas tanks in Mexico City in 1984, attract international attention, and most smaller-scale accidents do not even attract notice from a national press. In the USA, several quasi-official groups attempt to monitor accidents – the Acute Hazardous Events Data Base (AHE/DB) and the National Response Center of the Department of Transportation among them – but few other countries have systems for tracking industrial accidents.

What we do know about industrial accidents is that they are no accident. They have come to be accepted adjuncts of an industrial culture that, using materials of ever-greater toxicity, is extending its reach around the world.

Sources for map and commentary:
Gittus, J.H., et al, *The Chernobyl Accident and Its Consequences*, London: UKAEA, 1988; Kasperson, Roger, et al, *Corporate Management of Health and Safety Hazards: A Comparison of Current Practice*, Boulder, CO: Westview Press, 1988; Kleindorfer, Paul & Howard Kunreuther, *Insuring and Managing Hazardous Risks: From Seveso to Bhopal and Beyond*, Berlin: Springer, 1987; Lagadec, Patrick, *Major Technological Risk: An Assessment of Industrial Disasters*, Oxford: Pergamon Press, 1982; Organization for Economic Cooperation and Development (OECD), *OECD Environmental Data Compendium, 1989*, Paris: OECD, 1989; press reports, 1988-90; United Nations Environment Programme (UNEP), *Environmental Data Report* 2nd ed. 1989-90, Oxford: Blackwell, 1989.

27 TOXIC TRADE

Industrialized countries produce over 300 million tonnes of hazardous waste each year. These wastes pose a threat to human and animal health and any number of towns and ecosystems around the world have been poisoned by improper disposal of toxins. The dilemma of toxic waste is that there is really no 'proper' or safe way to dispose of it; if dumped in landfills or storage pits, poisons almost inevitably leak out into drinking water and residential areas; if burned, it leaves toxic residue; if dumped at sea (now banned by most countries), it threatens marine mammal and fish life. In lieu of solving the waste problem, many governments and private firms have chosen simply to ship the problem away – out of sight, out of mind. Poor countries are targeted to be recipients of the rich world's industrial waste – they need the revenue that dumping contracts can provide, and they often do not have the resources independently to assess the potential health and pollution effects of the waste they accept.

Between 1986 and 1988, over three million tonnes of waste were known to be shipped from rich to poor countries. This figure represents the tip of the iceberg; much of the trade is illicit or illegal, and its actual extent is difficult to determine. The international waste disposal business is a shady one: in many cases toxic shipments have been illegally dumped on the shores of poor countries; in other cases, governments of Third World countries are deliberately misled about the nature of proposed shipments.

The toxic trade has roused Third World anger – such countries have no interest in being the rich world's dumping ground – and almost 40 countries, mostly in the Third World, have now banned toxic waste shipments.

In addition to the Third World dumping trade, many industrialized countries exchange waste, although the flow of trade still reflects power imbalances between exporters and importers. Canada **117** receives a large share of US toxic waste; East Germany, Hungary and the UK are major repositories for European waste; China accepts waste from the USA and from Europe. This trade may be more consensual than Third World dumping, but it is no less dangerous.

Sources for map and commentary:

Organization for Economic Cooperation and Development (OECD), *OECD Environmental Data Compendium, 1989*, Paris: OECD, 1989; Vallette, Jim, *The International Trade in Wastes: A Greenpeace Inventory*, Washington DC: Greenpeace, 1989.

28 HOLES IN THE SKY

A thin layer of ozone, high in the stratosphere, acts as a shield against harmful solar ultraviolet radiation. A reduction in ozone allows more ultraviolet radiation to reach the earth. This is likely to result in long-term increases in skin cancers and damage to the human immune system. It will also lead to disruption of agriculture, reductions in crop yields, and possible large-scale alterations in a number of ecosystems. Ozone depletion is already a considerable and growing problem; the rate of destruction is so extensive that 'holes' in the ozone layer – varying in size, depending on the time of year - have formed over and close to the polar regions.

Since the mid-1970s, scientists have known that chlorine from synthetic compounds called CFCs (chlorofluorocarbons), and to a lesser extent a number of other chemicals, destroy ozone in the stratosphere. CFCs are entirely artificial compounds – they were developed in the 1930s and since then have been the basis of very powerful and profitable chemical industries. For many years, these industries, as well as governments in CFC-producing countries, dismissed theories of ozone depletion and resisted increasingly urgent calls from the scientific community for curbs in the production of CFCs and other ozone-depleting chemicals. The connection is now accepted, however, and the weight of opinion has finally shifted.

Agreement on the most appropriate and rapid solution is more difficult to achieve. The Montreal Protocol represents a first step. It was first signed in 1987 by 24 countries; by the end of 1989 it had been signed by 48 countries and agreed to in principle by another nine non-ratifying states (although ratification usually follows quickly, it cannot be assumed). Ratifying countries in the industrialized world agree to freeze CFC production at 1986 levels, with allowances for continued growth in the Third World for ten more years. While this agreement is a major step forward, environmentalists consider that it falls far short of what is necessary. The Montreal Protocol does not stop CFC production and ozone depletion – it merely slows down the pace of acceleration.

The US Environmental Protection Agency estimates that each 2.5 percent increase in CFCs causes an additional one million skin cancers, which will result in 20,000 additional deaths over the lifetime of the existing US population. Since the 1960s, CFC production has increased at an average 5 percent per year. In the mid-1980s, worldwide CFC production was over one million tonnes per year. The USA is the world's largest producer (and consumer).; in Europe, the UK is the largest producer. The uses of CFCs vary; in Europe aerosols account for 37 percent of CFC use; in the USA, 39 percent of all CFCs are used in motor vehicle air-conditioning and refrigeration. Globally, aerosols are the largest source of CFC emissions.

Sources for map and commentary:

US Environmental Protection Agency, *Effects of Changes in Stratospheric Ozone and Global Climate*, Washington DC: 1986; Hammit, J., *Product Uses and Market Trends for Potential Ozone-Depleting Substances, 1985-2000*, Santa Monica, CA: Rand Corporation, 1986; ozone hole graphics from the NASA Ozone Trends Panel, 1989, courtesy John Gille, National Center for Atmospheric Research, Boulder, CO; Shea, Cynthia Pollock. 'Protecting the Ozone Layer' in Worldwatch Institute, *State of the World: 1989*, New York: Norton, 1989; United Nations Environment Programme, *The Ozone Layer*, Nairobi: UNEP, 1987.

29 WAR-WASTED LANDS

Despite an encouraging number of ceasefires, peace talks and arms control talks, warfare was still widespread in 1989, affecting nearly a fifth of the world's states. Since 1945, most warfare has taken place in the 'Third World', and most wars raging in the late 1980s were civil wars. There is no universally accepted definition of war. This map includes wars defined politically – armed unrest involving quasi-military structures, as in Northern Ireland – as well as wars defined by high death tolls.

Wars are acutely destructive to the environment. Often, as in Vietnam in the 1960s and 1970s and in Central America in the 1980s, the natural environment is itself a military target. In Nicaragua, the US-backed contras made targets not only of the environment, but of environmentalists. Between 1982 and 1989, contras are known to have killed 30 environmental workers and kidnapped 70 more, forcing the closure of several national parks and halting several water pollution control projects. The largest contiguous area of unspoiled rainforest in Central America is to be found in Guatemala; by the late 1980s, one-third of Guatemala had been sprayed with defoliants as part of the government's anti-insurgency campaign, and also as part of the US-initiated 'war against drugs'. In the Vietnam war, US herbicide teams dumped millions of gallons of herbicides and defoliants (chief among them the now-notorious Agent Orange) over half the forests in the country; more than 50 per cent of the coastal mangrove swamps in the south were destroyed by bombs, defoliants, napalm, and bulldozers, and most will never regenerate. In the Iran-Iraq war, major wetlands were destroyed by bombing, chemical exposure and deliberately-set fires.

Even when the environment is not a designated target, it inevitably suffers. Agricultural areas become unworkable as villages are destroyed, farming families are killed or forced to flee, crops and livestock are seized or destroyed. And as in Afghanistan, large tracts of land are strewn with mines or with unexploded bombs and shells.

The environmental effects of war are rarely documented systematically, and thus this map can only suggest the nature and extent of the problem.

Sources for map and commentary:
Environmental Project on Central America (EPOCA), Green Paper Series, 1985 to present, Earth Island Institute, California; Stockholm International Peace Research Institute (SIPRI), *World Armaments and Disarmament: SIPRI Yearbook*, 1987, 1988, 1989, Oxford, OUP; Sivard, Ruth Leger, *World Military and Social Expenditures 1989*, Washington DC: World Priorities Inc., 1989; Wallensteen, Peter, ed., *States in Armed Conflict 1988*, Uppsala University: Department of Peace and Conflict Research, Report no. 30, July 1989.

30 NUCLEAR BLIGHT

In the late 1980s, the world nuclear weapons stockpile was approximately 50,000 warheads, about 16,000 of which are deployed at sea. Only five states acknowledge possession of nuclear weapons, although Israel and South Africa are also widely believed to be nuclear states. A number of other states allied with the USA and the USSR have nuclear weapons based on their territories, willingly or not. The development, production, storage, transport and deployment of nuclear weapons requires an extensive support network of bases and facilities, each one of which poses a permanent environmental hazard.

Recent revelations in the US media underscore the chronic nuclear pollution and heavy environmental damage caused by military nuclear facilities. Leaks of radioactive materials from the Rocky Flats facility threaten the drinking water supply of Denver; the Fernald materials production plant in Ohio has released more than 300 tonnes of uranium dust into the surrounding air and water; the agricultural land around Hanford, Washington, shows high levels of radiation.

In addition to chronic nuclear pollution, there are dozens of accidents each year involving military storage and transport of nuclear weapons or material. In this map, we focus on the most serious, known, nuclear accidents at sea – in which either nuclear reactors and/or nuclear weapons have been lost. Many more accidents may have happened but been kept secret. There are currently **119** about 50 nuclear weapons and seven nuclear reactors known to be resting on the ocean floor.

There would be even more nuclear material dumped at sea without strong international opposition. As recently as 1989, the British government was proposing to dump its nuclear submarines on the sea-bed once they are obsolete. The US government has officially rejected sea dumping as an option for getting rid of old nuclear military equipment, but the current administration is known to be reconsidering this possibility. France, the UK and the USA oppose a permanent ban on dumping although non-nuclear states are almost universally in favour.

The Pacific Islands have borne the greatest brunt of nuclear might and nuclear blight. Long used as nuclear testing grounds by France, the UK and the USA, whole island chains in the Pacific have been 'vaporised', while others are so radioactive as to be uninhabitable for thousands of years. The populations of many Pacific territories have become nuclear refugees. The Pacific nuclear-free movement, largely a women's movement, is now one of the most active grassroots anti-nuclear campaigns in the world.

Sources for map and commentary:

Arkin, William & Joshua Handler, *Naval Accidents 1945-1988*, Neptune Papers no. 3, Washington DC: Greenpeace/Institute for Policy Studies, 1989; Arkin, William & Richard W. Fieldhouse, *Nuclear Battlefields*, Cambridge, MA: Ballinger, 1985; Kidron, Michael & Dan Smith, *The War Atlas*, London: Pan; New York: Simon & Schuster, 1983; Radioactive Waste Campaign, *Deadly Defense*, New York: RWC, 1988; Stockholm International Peace Research Institute (SIPRI), *World Armaments and Disarmament: SIPRI Yearbook*, 1968/69, 1974, 1975, 1985, 1989, London: Taylor & Francis; Oxford, OUP.

31 AUTO CULTURE

In much of the world, most people still rely on bicycles, public buses and trains, animal-drawn carts and their own feet for transport. But the global trend is clearly towards automobile-centred transport.

The costs are high. Private automobiles clog the streets of most world cities bringing urban services to a standstill; expanding road networks gobble up scarce space and degrade agricultural land, especially in developments on the outskirts of cities; the fuel demands of private transport deplete fossil fuel resources. Worldwide, at least a third of an average city's land is devoted to roads, parking, and other car-related infrastructures. One of the most serious consequences is that cars play a prominent role in generating virtually all the major air pollutants (see Maps 17 and 23). In OECD countries, for example, 75% of carbon monoxide emissions, 48% of nitrogen oxides and 13% of atmospheric particulates (dirt and dust) are produced by cars and trucks; in the USA, motor vehicles are responsible for about 70% of total carbon monoxide emissions, 40% of nitrogen oxides, and 20% of particulates. Lead pollution, a serious health problem in most cities, is largely attributable to motor vehicle emissions.

The growing emphasis on private car ownership usually comes at the cost of public transport. Governments often assign priority to private motorized travel in traffic planning, budget decisions, and urban design. As the emphasis on private transport increases, funding and planning for public transit declines proportionally. This has the effect of further marginalizing people on the economic and social fringes of society – the poor, the elderly and, especially, women of all classes and ages. Women everywhere in the world are much more dependent on public transport since they are less likely than men to own private automobiles. A survey taken in London in the mid-1980s, for example, established that men drive cars twice as often as women, only a third of British women have a driving licence and 70 percent do not have a car. Automobile ownership both reflects and reinforces social inequities. The social structures that promote and reward car ownership will need to change if we are to be serious about environmental protection.

The global growth in private automobile production and ownership is fueled by automobile manufacturers who have a vested interest in the continuous expansion of their markets. As rich countries become saturated with automobiles, the Third World beckons as the next promising market. Car culture already has a firm grip on the large cities of Mexico, Brazil, and India, and is making strong inroads almost everywhere else in the developing world.

This map includes only information on cars. In some countries, such as China, the number of trucks and buses exceeds the number of cars and these, too, must be considered as major contributors to urban clog and air pollution.

Sources for map and commentary:
Mick Hamer, 'Men have Wheels While Women have Feet', *New Statesman*, May 24, 1985; Stan Luger, 'Stagnant Politics, Dirty Air', *In These Times*, December 13-19, 1989; Motor Vehicle Manufacturers' Association, *World Motor Vehicle Data: 1989*, New York, 1989; Michael Renner, 'Rethinking Transportation', Worldwatch Institute, *State of the World: 1989*, New York: Norton, 1989.

32 TOURIST TRAPS

By the mid-1980s, the global tourism business employed more people than the global oil industry; by the end of this century, tourism will be the world's largest economic activity. Tourism is increasingly the largest single revenue source for poor countries, and most governments actively promote the development of tourist trade. Without tourism, the economies of many of the Caribbean nations, for example, would collapse, as would the economies of many Mediterranean coastal towns.

The ratio of tourists to residents is a guide to the strain which tourists place on their host environment. High rates of tourism can overwhelm water supply, sewage treatment and municipal refuse facilities. St. Maartens, a small island in the Netherlands Antilles, receives the equivalent of its own population in tourists every 10 days. Tourist traffic and its related infrastructure can be a serious threat to fragile environments and often wipes out natural habitats entirely. To serve the tourist trade, many governments have embarked on ambitious programmes of road, airport, and hotel construction, often without serious regard for the environmental consequences of these developments. The wildlife trade, which threatens many rare species (see Map 33) often flourishes with tourism: rare and exotic birds and animals are hunted to sell to tourists – either alive, or as ivory trinkets, tortoise-shell combs, stuffed-toys made of animal fur, brilliantly-coloured corals, and the like.

The figures on tourism, collected by the World Tourism Office, monitor visitor arrivals. These include arrivals by guest workers or multiple border crossings by the same person or family. A few countries, Hungary for example, thereby appear to receive more tourists than they do in reality.

Another niche in the market has been spotted and tourism is now being heralded as a potential force for environmental good. The development of national parks and game reserves in many countries, most noticeably in Costa Rica and a number of African countries, is spurred on by the lure of tourist revenue. But present evidence suggests at best an uneasy coexistence of 'eco-tourism' and environmental protection.

Sources for map and commentary:
Commission of the European Communities, *Quality of Bathing Water: 1987*, Luxembourg: 1989; Enloe, Cynthia, *Bananas, Beaches and Bases: Making Feminist Sense of International Politics*, London: Pandora Press, 1989; World Tourism Organization, *Yearbook of Tourist Statistics: 1988*, Geneva, 1989.

33 WILD TRADE

Statistics on the extent of the traffic in wildlife are, at best, unreliable. An international body, the Convention on International Trade in Endangered Species (CITES) monitors the trade, and imposes restraints on the trade in certain animals designated for protection. Currently, trade is officially banned for about 675 species (identified as 'Appendix I' species), and regulated for at least 27,000 more ('Appendix II' species). CITES figures are the best available, but are known to be underestimates. Although CITES does make estimates of the scope of illegal trade, it is almost **121** impossible to verify these figures; the information presented on this map refers to both legal and illegal trade, although it must be assumed that most illegal trade is not reported. The representation of CITES statistics on this map includes the secondary trade in processed animal products and the re-export traffic – thus some countries are identified as both major exporters and importers of the same animals.

For the two inset maps, on the top 12 ivory and wildcat fur trading countries, we have used total trade by volume, both import and export, for the mid-1980s.

The trade in wildlife is almost entirely a luxury trade: the demand comes from rich countries, the supply from poor countries. The trade rests on a triad of commodification, greed, and desperation. To the brokers in wealthier countries, animals are mere commodities, exotic 'things' to be traded as expensive baubles. It is difficult to interpret the selling of wildlife, often pursued to the brink of extinction, as anything other than a sign of desperation. The closest parallel is perhaps prostitution; in extreme poverty, all the sellers have left to sell is themselves. In many poor countries, wildlife is what there is left to sell.

The traffic in animals is also a male enterprise. It is mostly men who poach the animals in poor countries; or men who organize expensive hunting safaris from rich countries; it is men who act as brokers of the international trade; and it is men who purchase the animals and their by-products: rhinos for aphrodisiacs, for example; or elephants, for ivory-handled daggers.

The traffic in wildlife is big business. The annual legal trade is worth about US$5 billion annually, and illegal trade is estimated at another $2 billion. In one year alone, 1985, the known trade included 43,000 primates, almost 9 million reptile skins, and 720 tonnes of ivory. While animal counts are imprecise, it appears that the trade in wildlife, dead and alive, has reduced the number of snow leopards left in the world to about 500, reduced tiger populations in India from about 40,000 to less than 3000, precipitated a decline in world rhino numbers of 70 percent since 1970, and reduced the herds of African elephants to about 625,000 out of an original population of over two million. It is widely thought that the only hope for preventing extinction of the elephant may be an absolute ban on ivory production and consumption. In 1989, the CITES countries (see pages 90-97) voted to do just this, but some African countries, such as South Africa and Zimbabwe, claim that their managed herds offer greater protection. CITES has been unable to persuade Hong Kong from selling its vast stockpile of imported ivory, though this is known to encourage illegal poaching.

Sources for map and commentary:
IUCN Conservation Monitoring Centre, *Red List of Threatened Animals*, Cambridge: IUCN, 1988; United Nations Environment Programme (UNEP), *UNEP News*, December 1989; World Resources Institute/International Institute for Environment and Development, *World Resources 1988-89*, New York: Basic Books, 1988.

34 HUNTING

Comparatively few human populations meet their food and clothing needs by hunting any more; and among those that do, their subsistence hunting leaves relatively little mark on the ecosystem. This map focuses on recreational hunting, whether for 'sport' alone or to supply the luxury trade in wildlife (see Map 33).

The primary source of information on animal extinctions is the IUCN's *Red List of Threatened Animals* which is published every two years. Species extinctions are often caused by a number of stress factors, such as habitat loss combined with over-hunting. The species identified on this map are those for whom the primary threat appears to be luxury or sport hunting.

Recreational hunters often defend their sport by saying that it is a celebration of nature, but the record speaks otherwise. Around the world recreational hunting has pushed hundreds of species to the brink of extinction and, over recent history, hundreds more have been hunted out of existence. Some species, shown on the map as endangered, are virtually extinct already. For example, by 1990 over much of eastern Africa, there were only 55 remaining Java rhino, about 800 Kemp's ridley turtles and fewer than a thousand black rhinos.

Despite repeated calls by the international community for an end to whaling, five countries still hunt whales. Whaling is conducted by these countries under the pretext of 'gathering scientific information' on whale populations, but in fact whaling is still the basis of a small but thriving commercial enterprise.

Hunting is big business. Apart from the fantastic sums of money sometimes paid for trophy hunting of rare animals (or merely parts, such as gorilla's paw or rhino horn), the ordinary business of hunting generates considerable revenues. Hunters in the USA spend around US$16 billion a year on fees and equipment. In poorer countries, hunting is often a major source of external revenue earned from rich foreigners. In 1983, Zimbabwe for example, earned US$6.2 million in fees and licenses from hunting for sport. Yet given the damage they do and the revenue that is generated, surprisingly few people hunt: in the USA, 7%; in Western Europe, 2%, in the USSR, 1%. Everywhere hunting is primarily a men's activity, and may often be construed as a rite of passage into manhood.

Sources for map and commentary:
Burton, J.A. and B. Pearson, *Rare Mammals of the World*, New York: Collins, 1987; Fitter, R., *Wildlife for Man*, New York: Collins, 1986; Inskipp, T. & S. Wells, *International Trade in Wildlife*, London: Earthscan, 1979; IUCN Conservation Monitoring Centre, *Red List of Threatened Animals*, Cambridge: IUCN, 1988; Organization for Economic Cooperation and Development (OECD), *OECD Environmental Data Compendium, 1989*, Paris: OECD, 1989; World Resources Institute/International Institute for Environment and Development, *World Resources 1988-89*, New York: Basic Books, 1988.

35 THE TIMBER TRADE

The tropical forests of the world are rich in highly-prized, 'luxury' woods such as teak, mahogany and balsa, among dozens of others. Extracting this timber is a high- profit, fast-moving big business. Most commercial logging operations in the tropics are monopolized by a handful of multinational timber conglomerates based in France, West Germany, the UK and Japan. They follow in the footsteps of the colonial traders in tropical timber, and in many ways replicate patterns of colonial exploitation – marked by utter disregard for the environment of Third World countries, perceived primarily as suppliers of raw materials to meet the 'refined tastes of the 'developed' world.

Uncontrolled logging has left many tropical forests in critical condition. Deforestation has already become a major problem in some of the earliest centres of commercial logging. Thailand, for example, once a major exporter, became a net importer of wood in 1980. Nigeria is virtually logged out. Many forests in Southeast Asia and West Africa are in a critical condition. Of the 56 timber-exporting countries, 23 are now net importers.

Timber is a valuable commodity of wide commercial interest - so valuable that the statistics are considered to be privileged commercial intelligence and are not widely available to the public. Independent environmental groups, particularly the UK-based Friends of the Earth, appear to have the most comprehensive accessible data on both the timber trade and the state of tropical forests. The International Tropical Timber Organization, formed in 1987 and based in Japan, is currently the only international body with oversight of the timber trade, but this organization's close ties with industry make suspect its effectiveness as an independent monitoring agency.

Sources for map and commentary:
Myers, Norman & Richard A. Houghton, *Deforestation Rates in Tropical Forests, and Their Climatic Implications*, London: Friends of the Earth, 1989; Nectoux, F. & Nigel Dudley, *The Hardwood Story*, London: Friends of the Earth / WWF 1987.

36 PAYING THE PRICE

In the course of an ordinary day, which many us live in a fog of pollution, we encounter a barrage of harmful chemicals, most of them invisible and many of them unknown – in our workplaces, on the streets, in our food and in our homes. In much of the world, air and water quality are, at best, suspect. That environmental derangement on this scale brings with it severe health repercussions cannot be doubted. As environmental damage escalates, so, too, will problems of health. However, **123** specific and definitive links are often difficult to establish. As yet, only a few environmental problems are known to have identifiable health consequences - such as the depletion of the ozone layer (see Map 28) causing rising rates of skin cancer. However, the hazards of urban living are clearly illustrated by increased lead levels found in the blood of most inhabitants of most large cities.

Exposure to carcinogenic chemicals and low-level radiation are the two principal causes of cancer and there has been little action to limit either. It is thus not surprising that, worldwide, cancer rates are rising – the World Health Organization reports six milion new cancer cases each year.

Lung cancer, the most common cancer in the developed world, is known to be caused by a number of factors, including occupational hazards and chemical exposures, but its primary cause is smoking. Tobacco fuels an extremely profitable and commercially aggressive industry. As rates of smoking decline in many industrial countries, tobacco firms are now exerting heavy pressure on Third World consumers, especially women, to take up smoking. Trends in lung cancer follow trends in smoking habits. As the lifestyles and environmental problems of the industrial world spread around the globe, so does lung cancer.

The increasing use of tobacco in many parts of the world has important implications for the environment. As a lucrative cash crop, tobacco is replacing traditional and subsistence crops in many Third World countries. Tobacco depletes soil nutrients and encourages heavy use of fertilizers and herbicides. Further, the World Health Organization estimates that one tree in six is cut for use in curing tobacco.

Health statistics are fairly complete for the industrial world, and unavailable or inconsistently available for most of the rest of the world. In any case, internationally available health statistics are not presented in conjunction with any discussion or evidence of contributing causes. Environmental causality, which must be superimposed on the raw health data, is usually best illustrated on the level of very specific and very closely-analysed case studies, not on a national or global level.

Sources for map and commentary:

Vahter, Marie, *Assessment of Human Exposure to Lead and Cadmium through Biological Monitoring*, Stockholm: UNEP, 1982; World Health Organization (WHO), *World Health Statistics*, 1988.

37 A CLASH OF INTERESTS

The global environment is a commons, shared by all countries. Increasingly, countries also share in its deterioration. Most pollution and degradation of the environment cannot be contained within national borders. Acid rain from the rest of Europe is devastating Sweden's forests and lakes; water diversion plans for irrigation in Ethiopia will diminish Egypt's water supplies; deforestation in Nepal, China, Bhutan and India has increased the frequency and extent of destructive flooding in Bangladesh. An estimated 40 percent of the world's population depends, for drinking water, irrigation or hydro power, on major river systems shared by two or more countries; in some cases, waterways are shared by as many as five or more countries.

In most cases, this share-out of environmental problems is inevitable. Occasionally, though, governments and private industries take active measures to 'ship' their pollution abroad. They may build smokestacks tall enough to disperse airborne pollutants, for example, or export unwanted and hazardous waste to poorer countries.

Increasingly, relations between governments are mediated by environmental issues. As certain resources are diminished and transboundary pollution increases, the environment is moving closer to the centre of international relations. Similarly, as individuals become more informed about environmental issues, national governments are judged on the efficacy of their environmental programmes. 'Green consciousness' poses a challenge to traditional notions of national sovereignty and international diplomacy, and to established forms of governance.

Sources for map and commentary:

Press reports; Renner, Michael, *National Security: The Economic and Environmental Dimensions*, Washington DC: Worldwatch Paper no. 89, May 1989.

INDEX

Acid rain, 62-63; 115-116
   disputes over, 88-89

Agriculture, 30-31; 104; 106
   chemicals, 32-33; 104-105
   soil suitability, 30-31; 36-37
   water use, 26-27

Air quality, 48-49; 110

Amazon Basin
   dam construction, 54-55
   rainforest loss, 24-25

Animals *see* Wildlife

Automobiles *see* Cars

Beaches, 78-79

Birds
   extinction threats, 20-21; 100
   hunting, 82-83, 100
   trade in, 80-81
   wetlands loss, 42-43

Cancer
   lung cancer rates, 86-87; 124
   carcinogen releases, 64-65

Carbon dioxide
   emission levels, 60-61, 115
   global warming, 16-17; 99

Cars
   pollution caused by, 48-49; 120
   manufacturers, 76-77
   number of, 76-77; 90-98 (table); 120

Central America
   environmental destruction from war,
   72-73

CFCs (chlorofluorocarbons)
   and greenhouse effect, 16-17
   consumption, 70-71
   ozone depletion, 70-71; 118

C.I.T.E.S., 90-98 (table)

Cities, 40-41; 107
   air quality, 48-49
   lead levels in blood of residents,
   86-87

Coal
   share of global energy, 50-51

Dams, 54-55; 113

Deforestation, 24-25; 84-85; 104

Desertification, 36-37; 106

Dirt and dust, 48-49

Driftnet fishing, 38-39
   disputes over, 88-89

Drinking water *see* Water quality

Drought, 28-29

Endangered species
   regulation of, *see* C.I.T.E.S.
   see also Extinctions

Electricity
   nuclear power, 52-53
   hydro power, 54-55

Energy
   consumption, 50-51; 110-111
   pollution, 60-61
   sources of, 50-51
   see also Firewood; Hydro power;
   Nuclear power; Oil

Erosion, 36-37; 106

Extinctions
   caused by hunting, 82-83; 122
   of animals, 20-21; 100
   of birds, 20-21; 100
   of plants, 22-23; 101

Famine, 28-29

Fertilizers
   artificial, 32-33; 104-105

Firewood, 56-57; 113
   share of global energy, 50-51

Fish
   supplies, 38-39; 106-107

Fishing
   environmental disputes, 88-89
   major fishing grounds, 38-39

Food
   availability, 28-29; 103
   fish supplies, 38-39
   genetic resources, 34-35; 101; 105
   major crops, 34-35
   see also Agriculture

Forests
    acid rain damage, 62-63
    and environmental disputes, 88-89
    rainforest loss, 24-25; 101-102
    timber trade, 84-85; 123

Fossil fuels, 60-61; 115

Friends of the Earth
    worldwide offices, 90-98 (table)

Fuelwood see Firewood

Fur trade, 80-81

Genetic engineering, 34-35; 105-106

Genetic resources, 34-35, 105-106

Global warming, 16-17; 99
    and fossil fuels, 60-61

Green parties, 90-98 (table)

Greenhouse effect, 16-17; 99

Greenhouse gases, 16-17; 99

Greenpeace
    worldwide offices, 90-98 (table)

Habitat loss, 24-25
    wetlands, 42-43

Health, 86-87; 123-124
    uninhabitable zones, 64-65
    waterborne diseases, 26-27

Hunger see Food

Hunting, 82-83; 100

Hydro power, 54-55; 113
    shares of global energy, 50-51

Industry
    CFC production, 70-71
    industrial accidents, 58-59; 66-67;
    105; 114; 117
    industrial waste, 64-65
    water use, 26-27
    see also Cars; Oil

Ivory trade, 80-81; 122

Land
    agricultural, 30-31; 36-37; 106
    erosion, 36-37; 106
    Mexico City, 40-41

Logging see Forests; Deforestation

Mammals see Wildlife

Mangrove wetlands see Wetlands

Men
    and hunting, 100, 122
    and the wildlife trade, 121-122

Mexico City, 40-41

Militaries
    and environmental disputes, 88-89
    see also Central America;
    Nuclear issues; Wars

Montreal Protocol, 70-71; 90-98
    (table)

Nepal
    tourism in, 78-79

Nitrogen oxides
    air pollution, 48-49

Nuclear issues
    nuclear power, 50-51; 111-112
    disputes over, 88-89
    nuclear fuel cycle, 52-53
    military accidents, 74-75; 119-120
    military/civilian link, 111-112
    military facilities, 74-75; 119-120
    share of global energy, 50-51
    nuclear testing, 74-75
    nuclear waste, 112
    nuclear weapons, 74-75

Oceans
    environmental disputes, 88-89
    fishing grounds, 38-39
    industrial waste dumping, 64-65
    oil pollution, 58-59; 114
    sea-level rise, 16-17; 99
    sewage dumping, 46-47

Oil
    pollution, 58-59; 114
    share of global energy, 50-51

Ozone depletion, 70-71; 118

Pesticides, 32-33; 104-105

Plants
number of species, 22-23
extinction threats, 22-23; 101

Plastics
in waste stream, 108

Pollution
disputes over, 88-89
from agricultural chemicals, 104
from fossil fuels, 60-61; 115
from industry, 64-65
from oil, 58-59
from sewage, 46-47
of air, 48-49, 110
of beaches, 78-79
of fishing grounds, 38-39
of wetlands, 42-43

Populations
and environmental pressures,
99-100
growth rates, 18-19
projected, 18-19
size of, 18-19
urban, 40-41

Protected areas, 90-98 (table)

Protests, 88-89

Rainforests see Forests

Recycling, 44-45

Relocations of people, 54-55; 113

Reptiles
hunting, 82-83
skins, 80-81

Sewage, 46-47; 109

Smoking, 86-87; 124

Soil loss, 36-37; 106

Sulphur dioxide
acid rain, 62-63
air pollution, 48-49
emissions, 60-61

Timber trade, 84-85; 123

Tourism, 78-79; 121

Toxic chemicals
releases, 64-65

Toxic waste
exports, 68-69; 117-118

Tropical rainforests see Forests

Uranium, 52-53

Urban issues
air quality, 48-49
lead levels in blood of city
residents, 86-87
migrants, 107
population, 40-41

War, 28-29; 72-73; 119

Waste
exports of, 68-69; 117-118
household, 44-45; 108-109
industrial waste, 64-65; 116
ocean dumping, 46-47; 64-65
sewage, 46-47

Water quality
beach pollution, 78-79
drinking water, 26-27; 102
sewage pollution, 46-47; 109

Water supply, 26-27; 102
disputes over, 88-89

Water use, 26-27; 102-103

Wetlands, 42-43; 108

Whales, 82-83; 122-123

Wildlife
extinctions, 20-21; 82-83
habitat loss, 24-25
hunting, 82-83; 122-123
number of species, 20-21
and tourism, 121
trade in, 80-81; 122
see also Wetlands; Birds

Women
as collectors of firewood, 86-87
as urban migrants, 107
and transport, 120

Worldwide Fund for Nature (WWF),
90-98 (table)